AF421792

Teri Campos has been in the classroom, in building leadership, and in professional development for over forty years. Her doctorate from the University of Missouri is focused on improving math instruction using visual thinking strategies. STEM is a passion born from her analytical mind and endless curiosity. She loves the outdoors, solving puzzles, traveling, and spending time with her family and friends. Her future includes roaming National Parks in her RV with her husband, Chris, and dog, Jack.

This book is for classroom teachers that may not have been science majors, but are now required to teach STEM. Teachers often face obstacles of time, money, space, and/or lack of familiarity and will get tips on how to overcome them. It is dedicated to teachers that want to be role models of a growth mindset as they adopt their own and take the risk of teaching STEM.

Teri Campos

A Year of Engineering Fun for Beginning Classroom STEM

AUSTIN MACAULEY PUBLISHERS®

LONDON * CAMBRIDGE * NEW YORK * SHARJAH

Ordering Information
Quantity sales: Special discounts are available on quantity purchases by corporations, associations, and others. For details, contact the publisher at the address below.

Publisher's Cataloging-in-Publication data
Campos, Teri
A Year of Engineering Fun for Beginning Classroom STEM

ISBN 9798891550216 (Paperback)
ISBN 9798891550223 (ePub e-book)

Library of Congress Control Number: 2024909156

www.austinmacauley.com/us

First Published 2024
Austin Macauley Publishers LLC
40 Wall Street, 33rd Floor, Suite 3302
New York, NY 10005
USA

mail-usa@austinmacauley.com
+1 (646) 5125767

I would like to thank my daughter, Audrey, who helped me with editing because she is a wordsmith and my mom who upon hearing my classroom tales constantly says, "You should write a book."

Table of Contents

Chapter 1
Introduction

I have heard that everyone has a book in them. I hope that is true. *My* book is about education and teaching—teaching STEM (Science, Technology, Engineering, and Mathematics), more specifically. I have been in education all my life. First and foremost as a student, a true life-long learner. I have received my Bachelor's Degree in Elementary Education, a Master's Degree in Curriculum and Instruction, an Educational Specialist degree, and my Educational Doctorate. In addition, I have certification in Administration and Gifted Education.

Next, I experienced the educational world through the lens of a teacher, I have taught grades ranging from kindergarten through ninth grade. I have spent time in classrooms in rural, suburban, and urban settings, ranging from affluent communities to communities in poverty. My teaching career also includes seven years of instructional coaching and several years in administrative roles.

My most recent experience included writing STEM curriculum and training teachers to implement hands-on activities in a STEM lab setting for students aged kindergarten-sixth grade. Lastly, to round out my educational experience, I witnessed the education of my children and grandchildren from the perspective of a parent. In each of these experiences I was able to compare methods and ideologies of varying districts in regard to STEM, teaching strategies for STEM education, and its impact on students, educators, and stakeholders. Through it all, I have always found math and science to be my strengths and greatest interest. I naturally see things in this world through an analytical lens. STEM education allows me to take my natural talents and passions and apply it to the world—to help make it all make sense.

When I started college, computers were the mammoth size of a room, and now they sleekly fit in your pocket on your phone. When I started teaching, we had dial-up modems that took hours to connect to the internet. I recall it took several days to download an application from the internet to be the first teacher in space. Now there is 5G speed, whatever that means, but what I do know is that it only takes a matter of seconds to reach all around the globe as I research places to go on my next bucket list trip.

While many things have changed, fundamental ways to learn and explore our world have remained the same. For example: The Socratic Method—which must have started in Ancient Greece with Socrates—as he explored his world thousands of years ago through the method of asking questions instead of giving answers to stimulate critical thinking and to draw out ideas and underlying presuppositions.

Additionally, Einstein said, "It is important to never stop questioning." Initiating the conversation of learning with questions beginning with "what", like "What happened?" and "What were the differences between the prototypes? What were the similarities?" Then, the questions hit all the five W's and naturally evolve into questions beginning with "why", like "Why did that happen? Why did your team choose to do it that way?" I believe in this method wholeheartedly, so much so, that my dissertation for my doctorate is centered on asking questions—using visual thinking strategies, to better understand the connections between pictures and math. You will see each of the STEM challenges in this book require asking questions at every step. Especially during the discourse session that should happen after every STEM challenge is completed.

STEM has recently gained popularity and become a "buzzword" in education and in teacher training and development, as school leaders are finally realizing its importance. However, I have found teachers feel unprepared to apply STEM lessons and the teacher preparation courses and professional development are lacking resources. Hence, my motivation to write this book. I feel it is important for students to be equipped with an analytical compass that STEM fosters and want to equip teachers with a resource to do that. My goal with this book is to reach as many teachers as possible, as I truly believe in the power of education to change lives. I hope that with my concise writing style combined with applicable, ready-to-use STEM lessons and activities—the reader will be inspired to implement STEM in the classroom right away. They say the best learning is done by "doing"—and each of my engineering challenges, requires action. Students will learn by following the design process laid out in each chapter. Students will be able to follow the engineering design process to build towers, cars, boats, bridges, planes, catapults, mazes, houses, solar cookers, and more. Before we dive into each of these sets of engineering challenges, it is important to cover a few things, beginning with the purpose and definition of STEM.

The Definition and Purpose of STEM

This book is meant to encourage and mentor teachers in their STEM endeavors. I have been a mentor to young teachers just beginning their career as well as veterans that were wary to get involved with "that new STEM stuff front office wants us to do." Both sectors appreciated my input and inspired me to write this book to get some of my ideas out into the mainstream of educators. I have been an "S-T-M" teacher from day one, so it was an easy transition for me to add the "E", or "engineering", piece. Others like me, especially elementary schoolteachers, are three-fourths the way there also because they already teach math and science, and use technology. This book is also for them as they add the "E" and learn to put all the pieces together despite the obstacles. Any teacher can become a STEM teacher if they try and hopefully after reading this book will want to try.

STEM is an acronym known by most nowadays, and some even add an A to include art and call it STEAM. I like that endeavor too, and that may be my next book. Let us review the letter components of the acronym: S = Science, T = Technology, E = Engineering, and M = Mathematics. Each part can be a stand-alone class with its own curriculum, but when you purposely present students with a challenge to create something in which they must apply science and math concepts with a team that must work together to design and build a model that solves a problem then you have STEM. Science and math are components and are often considered STEM education because they are the bookends, but a true STEM challenge incorporates all the letters and what they stand for.

A true STEM challenge uses math and science to make sense of everything else. I thought for a long time that I taught STEM because I was a math and science instructional coach and I was contributing to the STEM field, but I did not include engineering. Now that I do the engineering piece, I can say I am a STEM teacher with more of a sense of authority. If you are a math or science teacher, you are contributing to the STEM field and that is wonderful and I appreciate all your efforts. What I am saying is that you will thoroughly enjoy adding the engineering piece because you will see your subject matter come to life as teams apply the concepts you have taught them. STEM integrates all subject matter at one time and fosters what many call the "soft skills".

The "S" in STEM is for science, which includes earth, life, and physical science, or really everything in the universe. Science is the explanation for observed phenomena. It is the answer to "why?" The word science conjures up bad memories for some and scares many teachers away because of technical terms, vocabulary, and concepts. Instead, teachers need to embrace what Carl Sagan said, "Science is a way of thinking much more than it is a body of knowledge." That way of thinking is curiosity and asking questions like, "What if I do this?" and then keeping the data to analyze and compare results to draw conclusions. Learning really sticks with students that learn a science concept by observing how it applies to certain building material and affects an end product as they attempt to engineer structures to solve problems. The scientific method is often called the inquiry method and inquiring minds want to know. If you have an inquiring mind you have the makings of a scientist.

"T" stands for technology. When most people hear "technology", they automatically think of computers and robots (which is definitely technology). In the world of STEM, however, it means anything that is manmade. The Framework for K-12 Science Education defines technology as "any modification of the natural world made to fulfill human needs or desires." Social Studies teachers call it "capital resources". Straws, pipe-cleaners, cardboard, and other materials that are readily available because of technology. Since every prototype requires materials, it is not difficult to include technology into a STEM challenge.

Another way to use technology while teaching STEM is when something happens that sparks the "why?" question, we look it up on the internet. Also in the planning stages, teachers can use the internet as a resource to look up the background math and science concepts in order to later teach the students during prototype testing or discourse. Students may also want to find out more about the foundational science and math principles learned along their journey through the challenge.

"E" stands for engineering. An engineer uses science, math, and technology to design and build machines, engines, systems, and structures. Students become the engineers as they design and build structures in challenges. In "STEM" engineering means that the design process is taught and followed. The process steps are: Problem-> Imagine->Design->Create->Test->Analyze. There will be more than this paragraph to explain it, but essentially, it begins with a question, problem, or challenge. The students are organized into teams to brainstorm different solutions, design and create a prototype, and test it following certain criteria and constraints. Finally, the team analyzes the prototype's performance to improve the attributes they found lacking in a redesign and reconstruction to be retested, again, and again. Each step of the process requires a different type of engineering skill and each student will find their strengths along the way. There are structural engineers, mechanical engineers, chemical engineers, electrical, industrial, and civil engineers and all are needed in different amounts in different stages of the different types of STEM challenges.

"M" stands for mathematics. Math includes data, geometry, computation, measuring, and everything you do with numbers and shapes. The list seems endless and generally age restrictive which is daunting to many teachers. I believe as Dean Schlicter does, "Go down deep enough into anything and you will find mathematics." Math is the answer to "how?" How far, how much, how many, how often? I remind students that Einstein said he was not any smarter than anyone else was; it was just that he stayed with the problems longer. That is the key. Never give up.

When doing a STEM challenge, a team should stay with a problem and its solution through at least two iterations. It is in the analysis and answering the new question, "What if we do this instead?" that stretches the minds and creativity of the team. Student engineers will use mathematics in every STEM challenge and may not even realize it. Some examples are, when they measure out materials and measure final prototypes because the challenge was to see who could build the tallest tower or longest bridge. Students use math when they adapt different angles or incorporate different shapes in the construction of towers, marble mazes, and other structures. Some challenges require the math of weighing, others require counting, and older students will use more complex math concepts when finding width to height ratios and the degrees of inclines.

STEM is about putting all these parts together. STEM is about reflecting on the science, math, and engineering concepts behind the challenge. Discourse is needed to highlight what science was used, what math was applied, what technology was needed, and how engineering was accomplished. There are many building block subjects, but the true STEM challenge puts it all together. I also believe that STEM challenges provide even more benefits and adds the bonus skills of collaboration, creativity, communication, and critical thinking. The 4 C's of STEM I will discuss in later parts of this book.

Still not ready to dive into some STEM challenges? I was in the classroom for many years and I feel there are some common obstacles or roadblocks to teaching STEM. Here are the ones that come to mind:

- Not enough time
- Not enough space
- Not enough materials
- Not orderly and neat, too messy
- Not really a core subject or state tested

- Not worth the effort
- Not in my wheelhouse because I teach… Language Arts, History, etc.

I will address these roadblocks and give my tips on how to overcome them. I have heard fellow teachers mention each of them and know they are real. It is not my intention to diminish how difficult it is to overcome obstacles in education and am aware there are many others that could be added. There are many unique situations, which I may not address and sometimes circumstances beyond our control. If you see yourself and your struggles in the roadblocks that I do address I hope you take my advice and begin your STEM journey. Be like Einstein and never give up.

This book begins your STEM journey with some hands-on activities to explicitly teach the engineering loop and the bonus team skills that are needed and improved by doing STEM challenges. The paper chain and pipe cleaner challenges are easy introductory activities. The needed materials are easy to obtain and the directions are easy to follow. It is a fun way to wade in rather than just jumping into the deep end. You have probably even done the pipe cleaner activity as team building in professional development, I use it with a STEM spin.

This book includes STEM challenges in nine categories and then variations in each that will provide a school years' worth of STEM challenges if you choose to do a month of Fridays building towers and then a month of engineering cars, and so forth. The engineering design loop is outlined in the first lesson plan of each category Problem-> Imagine->Design->Create->Test->Analyze and then three to four variations follow usually incorporating different construction materials. The variations are repeated following the outline of the first lesson with the intention of getting multiple iterations. New materials make it a new challenge because the properties of the new material will create new problems for the team.

The challenge categories are towers, cars, boats, bridges, catapults, planes, marble mazes, houses, and solar cookers. It is not required to do these categories in a structured order and you can do your favorite first. You can do just the first challenge in a category and then return to the category later in the school year, but the idea of a month spent doing each category supports the idea of depth by iteration. There is no magic way of presenting these challenges. I would suggest doing the solar cookers when it is sunny and warm outside unless you have access to a giant solarium. I truly believe that it is repeating a challenge, what we call iterations, where the magic does happen. Students will understand science and math concepts more deeply the second and third time they are exposed and it begins to make sense as they problem-solve in authentic situations.

The illustrations are rudimentary, but I wanted to include a visual of some examples of structures I have seen that were solutions created by students. I did not want photographs, but knew many teachers would need a visual to get some idea of possible solutions. I believe showing students a prototype or photograph prior to their own design step hinders their creativity. Most prototypes will depend on the material you have available and that limitation is okay as long as there is team equity. The drawings I include are meant to give teachers a beginning point for their journey, not a destination or single right answer.

Chapter 2
The Roadblocks

With any new endeavor, there are obstacles to overcome. There are the internal obstacles we face of self-confidence, and lacking previous experience. There are also external obstacles to overcome and I have identified some that are common across the classrooms and teachers I have encountered throughout my career. I know that the older you are the less you probably experienced STEM during your own educational foundation from the student perspective and that goes back to the internal foes. It is difficult to teach any material with which you are unfamiliar, but the beauty of STEM is that there is not one right answer or way to do things. Those that teach a growth mindset want students to take risks, so a teacher can be a good role model, as they adopt their own growth mindset and take the risk of teaching STEM even though they lack familiarity. The common roadblocks that teachers face that I will address are: time, space, materials, mess, and curriculum, not worth the effort or not in their wheelhouse.

Time

Teachers believe there is not enough time to teach STEM. There is not enough time in the school day to teach everything they are required to teach. Many feel that adding STEM is just one more thing on their already crowded plate. They feel pressure considering the entire scope of math and reading objectives that need to be taught in every grade level and science objectives in the select few. Many districts also require too much time testing and that again limits instructional time in the classroom. Time is the enemy for many things.

When a teacher does spend time for reflection discourse following a STEM challenge, there are cross-curricular connections that really utilizes that precious limited time because there are relevant applications of science and math concepts and that connection needs to be drawn out through questioning. It is the magic of the teaching craft to pull that out of students as you ask why their design worked or did not work the way they intended. Taking that extra 5-10 minutes of reflection is the reward for teachers when they see the metaphoric light bulbs go off as students figure it out for themselves. Teachers will find that one STEM challenge taught science, math, engineering, and communication arts all at the same time. That seems like a time-saver to me.

Planning is key and the ultimate time-saver. With the right planning STEM can be done in 10-50-minute blocks. It is easy to break challenges down into ten-minute chunks to fit any schedule. Time between the chunks also allows for an incubation of ideas for the students. It could also allow time to procure needed materials. There is time for students and teachers to go home and scrounge through the junk drawers and recycling bins for material. The STEM chunks of time follow the design process, Problem->Imagine->Design->Create->Test->Analyze. The first ten-minute chunk is the introduction of the problem or question and perhaps team selection, sort of like setting the stage as they imagine other ways that problem has been solved in the past.

Teachers can share the background information that explains how problems were solved throughout history and evolutions of different solutions, so they can imagine new ways to solve the problem. The second ten-minute chunk is for teams to collaborate by brainstorming design plans and sharing independent drawings to combine creativity into a team solution. The third ten-minute chunk is for gathering materials and team collaboration for prototype creation and construction. The fourth ten-minute chunk is for testing, analyzing, redesigning, and adapting the prototype with reconstruction. The fifth ten minutes is a final test, which usually turns into a friendly competition and involves quantifiable measurement or other math in some way.

The last ten minutes is the discussion of what happened throughout the week or throughout the challenge and is meant to illicit the science and math concepts and highlight the creativity and critical thinking that went on. It is sometimes easier to find five separate ten to fifteen minute chunks throughout the day or the week. Sometimes it is easier to save all the fun for a Friday afternoon and do all the chunks of the process at once in a fifty to sixty minute block. Try it both ways and see what works best for your schedule. Either way is time well spent.

Planning a STEM challenge that is a culmination of a particular area of study in math or science is a great idea. However, it does not hurt to do any challenge any time and review the math and science concepts that were used. Using a read-aloud book as the launcher for a STEM challenge appeals to the literacy minded teachers and students. It is one of the best ways to engage younger students and launch them into a challenge. Just look at the categories in this book and read-aloud books will pop into your mind that would be great introductory lessons. The category of towers brings to mind several picture books that you could read before starting a tower challenge. The same goes for the other categories of cars, boats, houses, planes, and bridges. There is a book series, *If I Built a ...* as well as others you probably already read and have in your classroom. Planning a STEM materials area in the classroom overlaps a Makers area or other learning stations usually found in elementary classrooms. Having materials on hand saves time and money and is addressed more fully in the other sections that follow.

A STEM challenge is a better use of time than other Fun Friday activities. Whether you teach five chunks, one each day of the week or all at once, the best day to culminate is Friday. Calling a STEM challenge, a Fun Friday activity tricks students into having a friendly competition that gets students busy having fun while learning at the same time. Planning is the key for many instructional successes and it is no different for STEM. Buying this book with ready-made STEM challenges will help with that planning and hopefully, save you some time.

Space

Another common roadblock is space. Many teachers suffer storage issues and space for peer collaboration. Not having enough space to work in teams for hands-on construction and design testing is a problem. I will tell you what I did to overcome the space issue in different ways, as each building is unique in compounding the problem and also in offering alternative solutions. Look for wide-open spaces that can be scheduled during open times. For example, I have worked with teams on community tables in cafeterias and libraries when they were not in use. I have worked with teams in the gym and hallways when they were vacant. I have used stage areas in older buildings. I have used playgrounds and outdoor classrooms weather permitting. Start looking around and scout out some potential spaces on your campus. Space is a problem at home too, think about what have you done to better utilize space there and adapt it to school.

Inside classrooms, it is important for group work in all subjects, not just STEM. Follow the same routines and procedures but with a STEM spin on them. The STEM teams can cluster around one desk during the brainstorming time. Space for other steps of the engineering loop will depend on the size of the materials and the end product. Some challenges need wide-open areas only on the testing chunk of the process, so you can do most of the challenge in your room and then carry the prototypes to that area for testing. Most classrooms have community areas that range from reading tables to area rugs that can be utilized during the collaboration and construction chunks of the process. Push the desks aside and work on the floor. Push the desks together and work in pods. Be a creative problem solver and you can find space to work.

Where to store prototypes may be another space obstacle if there is a large span of time between construction and testing. I have used tops of shelves, windowsills, the tops of library shelves, and unused classrooms, such as the traveling art or music teacher. (With permission, of course.) I even tied a string around a section of the prototype, pinned the other end of the string to the drop ceiling panel, and made prototype mobiles that hung above our heads until we needed them again. There should be explicit expectations to respect the work of others and not touch anything while being stored in community areas. It usually is not a problem because everyone has something at stake and are dependent on the compassion and cooperation of fellow classmates.

The actual space of storing engineering and Makers building and construction material is addressed in the following "Materials" section. I suggest you discuss the space problem with your colleagues and administration to hear their solution ideas. Every building presents its own architectural space problems, but also may offer its own unique solutions. Ask the building science teachers where they store the science fair exhibits and any teacher that is known for displaying student work that is more three-dimensional and requires volume storage.

One space-saver I created was a pyramid of bins for storage. I collected fifteen empty ice cream tubs from Baskin Robbins, which is my local ice cream shop. They would just normally throw them away, so it took a while, but I stopped by every couple of days to retrieve them. (I almost always bought ice cream too in the name of business partnership, of course.) I painted them a bright color and hot-glued them together into a pyramid of cubbies with a row of five then a row of four, three, two, and one. I put them on top of a built-in counter for easy access. One tub contained boxes of foil, wax paper, and plastic wrap, one contained old newspapers and paper towels, one bin was for craft sticks, toilet paper tubes, etc. This is what my pyramid of empty ice cream tubs looked like:

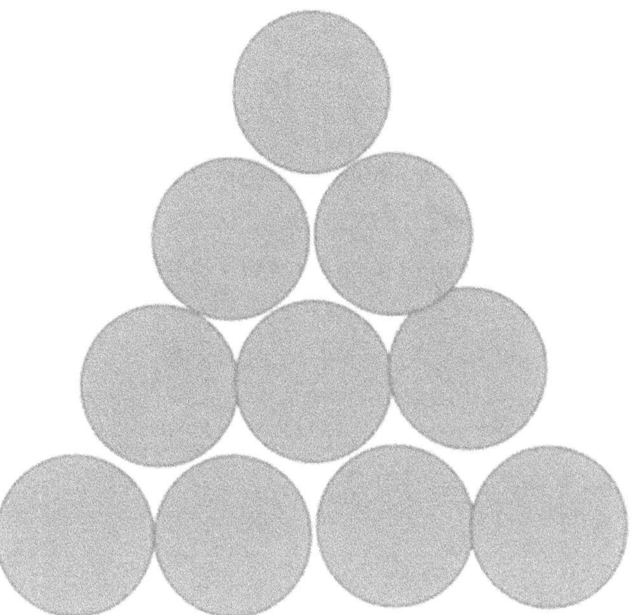

Materials

The materials obstacle is a cousin to the storage problem. It is great to have a lot of material, but can also be a curse if you lack storage space. Most teachers lack enough materials to teach their curriculum for an entire school year. Teachers are notorious for buying things for their students out of their own pocket and are frequent customers of the dollar store. Teachers in districts with a majority of low socio-economic families even buy paper, pencils, glue, notebooks, and basic school supplies whenever they can catch a sale at local stores. Most kindergarten classes run out of tissues before cold season even arrives. Not enough materials is a problem for many projects, not just STEM.

I have gotten fast food restaurants to donate cups and straws. I have gotten Target to donate a hundred dollars of art supplies. Look at your community and business partners to explore possible donations. Many schools have local entities that have "adopted" them and they are often looking for ways to help the school and its students. There are small grants available annually especially for consumable materials that need to be replenished yearly. When school districts change science texts often the old lab materials are discarded or stored in a district holding area, so be the first to claim them. There are social networks that help teachers get funding for special projects and a Makerspace or STEM supplies would be a very worthwhile project.

Collect shoeboxes, milk crates, and grocery boxes in which to store materials or to be broken down for building materials. Many of the items in your home recycling bin are great for STEM projects; just make sure they do not have sharp edges. When the material list has "recyclable or found objects" it will have you looking at your trash through a whole new lens. You will be able to think of a ton of new ways you can use this box or that container, etc. Here is a list of suggested materials to keep on hand that are free or very inexpensive. There needs to be paper, glue, tape, pencils, and scissors for most projects as well.

Material for a Makerspace or STEM:

-Tinker Toys, Legos, or K-nex, something to assemble and disassemble
-Magnets
-Wires, trash bag ties
-Play dough
-Clips, clothespins, paper clips
-Foil
-Pipe-cleaners
-Scissors
-Paper, construction paper, envelopes, playing cards
-Markers, crayons, pencils
-Paper tubes like from toilet paper and paper towels
-Toothpicks or skewers
-Tape (masking, duct, and clear)
-Glue (hot glue gun is nice, but make sure it does not get too hot)
-Stapler, staples, brads
-Rubber bands
-String, ribbon, yarn
-Popsicle sticks
-Plastic, Styrofoam, and paper cups
-Straws
-Egg cartons
-Tape measure, yardstick, rulers
-Cardboard, card stock, notecards
-Wood blocks
-Nails, screws, hammer, screwdrivers
-Washers
-Craft items like googly eyes, stickers, fabric, and buttons
-Cotton balls, cotton swabs

Each STEM challenge in this book has a list of materials highlighted. Plan ahead to ensure there will be enough materials on hand when needed. Substitutions are always possible due to the availability of resources. You can make homemade playdough with flour, salt and water if you lack ready-made. Remember to multiply by however many groups you have since the materials listed are for one group. Working in teams means that less material is needed since there can be material sets of 6-8 instead of 24 separate sets. Teamwork is mandatory for STEM challenges and that saves material in the long run, but there should always be equity between teams.

Messy

STEM is messy. Teachers as a whole do not feel comfortable giving up control. Cooperative learning is louder and messier than traditional learning in nice neat rows. It is up to the teacher to establish routines and procedures that create a type of organized chaos during cooperative learning. One important procedure to establish is to have a call-back-to-order like flicking the lights or counting down from 3 or my favorite, I say "M-I-Z" you say "Z-O-U", you could use any college chant. There are many ideas out there to try. If you already incorporate cooperative learning in your classroom then stick with what is familiar.

Having jobs for each team member saves time and limits movement. Supply retriever, timekeeper/structural engineer, and CEO, are my top three jobs and three is my favorite size of a team because it ensures that everyone stays engaged. Not every class size is evenly divisible by three, so a fourth job could be data collector who writes down pertinent information, for groups with three that responsibility falls to the CEO. It depends on space and supplies how many students need to be on each team. There are many ways to select teams, and with STEM random is okay, but it goes better when every team has at least one natural leader.

Having explicit step-by-step directions will increase order. The STEM challenges in this book include directions, but you can adapt them to your specific needs. Some challenges require a student proficient with measuring and all challenges require creativity and communication, so think of all the required skills when creating groups.

Having the materials counted out into neat piles for each group adds to order, but also adds to the time issue we addressed earlier. Depending on the age of students and classroom responsibilities, that job can be done by a student prior to STEM time, or done by the supply retriever during STEM time. The returning of materials afterward should also be orderly with the expectation that everything has a place and everything should be in its place when done in order to stay organized and to be able to find it next time it is needed. The supply retriever is also the supply returner, but all team members are custodians and have the clean-up responsibility.

Every challenge has safety suggestions. Many safety guidelines are common sense such as using scissors safely, but should be taught and enforced. The younger the student the more safety procedures need to be explicitly taught. Liquids require more diligence, but students are capable when taught the most efficient methods and trusted to follow safety rules. You should read the safety precautions aloud before you hand out materials and even demonstrate the proper use of any equipment that is being introduced for the first time. Safety is usually tied to mess, for example it is important to wipe up any spills immediately to avoid slips and other types of accidents.

Allow time for proper clean-up, but be flexible because some challenges require more time than others do. Whatever routines and procedures are established for science and other hands-on activities should work for STEM. Orderliness is dependent on procedure and planning the best flow for the needed movement helps keep things neat. I kept classroom expectations posted and referred to the posters often. It is a three-ring circus and you are the ringmaster. One common problem is that excitement often leads to noise and sporadic movement like students running for paper towels when there is a spill. And STEM challenges are exciting. Call the class back to order with your routine procedure and remind the class of expectations and time limits and do it as often as you deem necessary to keep the order at a maximum and the mess at a minimum.

Not a Core Subject

Teachers that believe STEM is not a core subject because there is not a STEM assessment need to look at the Next Generation Science Standards. It clearly states that the engineering design process is as equally important as the scientific inquiry process in all levels, kindergarten to grade 12. Of course, the process gets more sophisticated at higher levels. The Framework includes science and engineering practices. Here is a part of what it says:

"Engaging in the practices of engineering likewise helps students understand the work of engineers, as well as the links between engineering and science. Participation in these practices also helps students form an understanding of the crosscutting concepts and disciplinary ideas of science and engineering; moreover, it makes students' knowledge more meaningful and embeds it more deeply into their worldview. The actual doing of science or engineering can also pique students' curiosity, capture their interest, and motivate their continued study; the insights thus gained help them recognize that the work of scientists and engineers is a creative endeavor—one that has deeply affected the world they live in. Students may then recognize that science and engineering can contribute to meeting many of the major challenges that confront society today, such as generating sufficient energy, preventing and treating disease, maintaining supplies of fresh water and food, and addressing climate change."

Beginning in grades K-2, students learn that a situation people want to change can be thought of as a problem that can be solved. Then after thinking about the problem students sketch their ideas or make a physical model to meet the requirements of the problem. Then they compare different solutions by testing each one to see how well it solves a problem or achieves a goal based on how it functions.

In grades 3-5 specifying criteria and constraints is added. Criteria are requirements for a successful solution and any function that a design is expected to perform or qualities that would make it possible to choose the best design. Constraints are limitations that must be taken into account when creating the solution. In the classroom, common constraints are the materials that are available and the amount of time students have to work. Then they develop several alternative solutions and compare them systematically to see which is best by testing prototypes using controlled experiments like science inquiry, except the goal is to achieve the best possible design. Another way to improve designs is to build a structure and then test it until it fails and then redesigning the structure so that it is stronger. It teaches that "failure" is an essential part of the design process, as it points the way to better solutions.

In grades 6-8, the problem is defined more precisely and involves deeper thinking to consider the end user and side effects. The development of a prototype involves testing it with a matrix to combine good things of other designs and combining all the good parts while eliminating the bad. The redesign and retest steps may be done three or four times.

At the high school, level students are expected to engage with major global issues of science, technology, society and the environment. Defining the problem requires both qualitative and quantitative analysis. Designing the possible solutions requires prioritizing parts of the problem and making tradeoffs. Testing the solutions is more sophisticated. Students have to take into account criteria and constraints, anticipate possible societal and environmental impacts, and to test the validity of their solutions by comparison to the real world.

The NASA website defines the engineering design process as: Ask, Imagine, Plan, Create, Experiment, Improve, and go back to create and experiment or test in a loop. There are slight differences on the wording of the design process depending on where you look. Another example from teaching engineering is: Problem, Explore, Design, Create, Test, and then loop back to design, create, and retest. The STEM challenge steps in this book are a combination of these two. Problem->Imagine-> Design-> Create-> Test-> Analyze, and loop back to redesign, recreate, retest as often as time allows. Each team analyzes as they test in order to redesign. But I always end a challenge with a sharing and analyzing discussion with the entire class. All design processes are in essence the same with just different words.

Therefore, STEM is supposed to be a part of the science curriculum because of its engineering piece. Omitting engineering at any grade level creates problems for the following grade levels and creates a domino effect with missing foundational blocks. It is important to have engineering practiced each year of school for it to become more complex and build upon skills. I hope you use the STEM challenges in this book to introduce engineering to your students where they are and take them to the next level.

Not Worth the Effort

I have heard another complaint from teachers that it is just not worth their effort. It requires work for teachers to find the time, find or make space, obtain materials, and teach the engineering design process while maintaining order and protocol. I would argue that it is worth the effort because STEM teaches other skills as a by-product.

STEM teaches **critical thinking** skills and instills a passion for innovation. The section of this book called the 4 C's attempts to outline why teaching STEM is well worth the effort. Students need **communication** and **collaboration** skills in every subject. Another benefit obtained by doing STEM challenges is **creativity**. Yes, math and science are used in the engineering design process, but so are the 4 C's (critical thinking, communication, collaboration, and creativity) which gives you more bang for your buck.

If you are an elementary teacher, it is your responsibility to teach engineering, and STEM challenges are the best way to do that. Even if you only find time to do a STEM challenge once a month, that is better than just ignoring that part of your science curriculum. The benefits for students far outweigh the efforts teachers must endure to provide a quality STEM education.

STEM teaches children more than science and mathematics concepts. The hands-on learning with real-world applications helps develop a variety of the desired 21st century skills they list in the Next Generation Science Standards like productivity, social skills, flexibility and initiative. The skills of problem-solving, curiosity, decision-making, leadership, entrepreneurship, and acceptance of failure are some other benefits students gain from STEM education. Students also learn how to manage their time and break larger projects into smaller steps. That skill will help them throughout their lives, whether they find themselves later in life working on an office project or remodeling a house, or hopefully in a STEM related field.

Each STEM component brings a valuable contribution to a well-rounded education. Science gives students an understanding of the world around them. It helps them to become better at research and critical thinking. Technology prepares young people to work in our innovative high-tech world and how to be more resourceful. Engineering allows students to enhance problem-solving skills and apply knowledge in new projects. Mathematics enables students to analyze information, identify and eliminate errors, and make conscious decisions for solutions. STEM education integrates teaching and learning into a cohesive system.

Since STEM challenges are project-based learning and problem-solving, students form a mindset of flexibility and curiosity. Teamwork that is used in STEM fosters divergent thinking and collaboration. The testing of prototypes to the point of failure teaches students that it is part of a process and not the end of it. The failure gives them another chance to improve. Learning from mistakes is a life skill. It has also been found that experience in STEM activities has raised self-confidence for students and leads them to pursue STEM fields in higher education and future jobs. It helps students find out that math and science can be fun when they are exposed to positive interactions that apply those concepts that may have been only abstract before creating concrete structures while problem-solving along the way. Teachers that only prepare students for the world as it is now are not really preparing them for their future world.

Many studies have found that STEM challenges even the playing field for marginalized students like English language learners or those on IEP's. Many students that do not have success in regular pencil-and-paper tasks get to shine during hands-on activities. Many students have oral skills beyond their written capabilities and the communication and collaboration of a STEM challenge gives them that alternative, to talk instead of write. The engineering process can highlight creativity and give kids a chance to think outside of the box. Students that may avoid sharing in traditional whole-class lessons often take the lead in small group teams. Those that are mechanically inclined become the desired team member and appreciated for their ability to build when that ability may have been hidden prior to STEM.

Not in My Wheelhouse

Teachers that are more comfortable with language arts sometimes feel that STEM is not something they can teach confidently. Many teachers never experienced STEM during their own educational journey, so are now learning it as an adult. It is difficult to teach something that is alien to you. I have been a co-learner in my STEM journey as I learned alongside my students and it was sometimes very uncomfortable, but always rewarding. To overcome a lack of experience and confidence just takes a growth mindset. You do not know how to teach STEM

yet. However, you can and will with practice. Be the role model of a growth mindset. You know that corny saying, if you are not living on the edge you are taking up too much room.

Once you try a STEM challenge, you will find out what fun it is. Students will beg for more and even work to earn more STEM time. You may even begin to use it as a reward. What teacher can say that fun learning is not in their wheelhouse? Do the STEM challenge and then focus on the language arts benefits for students as they improve communication skills, learn how to collaborate more effectively, and gain creative and critical thinking opportunities? You can read the science and math background information aloud that is included in each STEM challenge to the class to let them digest that and see for themselves how it applies to their solution designs. Many Engineering Design processes include an "explore" or "research" step. I have provided that for each challenge as a time-saver, but you can assign that step to your students if time allows or you prefer.

As I have stated in previous sections, there are many skills learned through STEM challenges. The application of math and science to build prototypes and then test designs to find the best solution fosters collaboration, creativity, communication, and critical thinking. The next section will address the 4 C's more thoroughly. Critical thinking not only helps students do better in math and science, but it also improves their ability to analyze text, have deep discussions, and write essays which any language teacher would want. The true power of STEM learning is that it combines all subjects into a multi-disciplinary approach.

Chapter 3
The 4 C's of STEM

As I stated earlier, there are many by-products and extra rewards reaped from a STEM challenge. Students are expected to improve science and math skills when engaged in STEM because it says so right in the name. There are other skills that will also improve due to the inherent nature of a STEM challenge. The ones I want to highlight all begin with the letter "C", collaboration, creativity, communication, and critical thinking, thus the title of this chapter.

Collaboration

Collaboration is not just teamwork or group work, but a sharing of ideas when one is working on a STEM challenge. Too often with groups of children, there is parallel play and forced cooperation or compliance. For a team to be successful in accomplishing the challenge it is important that every person on the team thinks and works together and feels valued and respected. In addition, when that is not happening then there is communication procedures and accountability protocols to utilize in order to get there. A structured interdependence is the goal. Depending on the age of your students, it may serve you well to define collaboration with more than just the introductory lessons I provide in this book.

Scientists and engineers plan and carry out investigations in the field and in the laboratory collaboratively. Projects in the real world's workplace require the ability to work with others cohesively. Very few jobs are done in isolation, so when students learn how to work with others successfully they are more prepared and ready for college or a career. The social skills category on report cards similar to "works and plays well with others" comes to mind. It has been recognized as a desirable skill for a long time in education because I remember seeing that on my report cards from grade school eons ago.

Investigations in science and the design process in engineering are both systematic and can and should loop. They both have key steps, but can be done in different order or repeated in different ways when a step is not needed or combined with another. All team members have a say and should feel free to suggest time-saving tips as time is always a constraint when done during the school day organized by schedules. The process requires persistence in clarifying what counts as data and what they must keep a record of in order to stay on track. There should always be a data collector, but it is everyone on the team's responsibility to get numbers recorded accurately and organized.

The redesign step requires identifying variables and what can be changed and what cannot. Team members with scientific prowess will shine here. The checks and balances that occur between team members is a natural process when every member feels important in the decision-making and responsible for the end product. When team members feel invested and are engaged is collaboration at its best.

College and career readiness standards state that students should "prepare and participate effectively in a range of conversations and collaborations with diverse partners building on others' ideas and expressing their own clearly and persuasively." To achieve this, STEM team configuration should change for every new challenge in order for students to have the opportunity for more diversity in teams. Over time, every student in the class has the opportunity to work with every other student. Every STEM challenge should allow time for the students to think independently first and then to share ideas as a team member, so that each has had time to collect their own thoughts, but also can listen to others state persuasively why their idea might be better in some way.

Students will improve with practice. They should feel free to ask teammates to clarify and not feel defensive when they are asked to do so as well. If a student feels they have a better idea or plan then they must be able to explain or show why but should feel welcome and encouraged to do so. Learning to disagree and compromise is more difficult for some, but not impossible, and a desirable life skill.

Research has shown that collaboration helps students learn material more deeply and develop personal skills that last a lifetime. Just as there are Accountable Talk guidelines for elementary students, which will be reviewed in the communication section, there are norms for collaboration. The norms I find useful are from The Adaptive School 2008:

- Paraphrase often
- Ask questions
- Pause before responding
- Introduce new ideas
- Use data in discussions
- Be conscious of others and yourself
- Assume everyone's intentions are good

I would post these guidelines after explaining them, especially the more difficult concepts with simpler language. Paraphrase means that you can restate what you just heard or saw. Being conscious of others means that you have empathy and can relate to feelings and respond to social cues. Being conscious of yourself means that you know the impression you are giving others. Ask yourself if you are being loud or bossy or not open to ideas. Adjust your body language and facial expression to show that you are open and accepting of ideas other than your own. Assign roles randomly so that each student can feel what it is like to be the leader (CEO), the organizer, the recorder, and the materials retriever. Once a student has experienced each role they can have empathy for others that currently are assigned to that role and they may discover an aptitude they did not know they possessed.

Use the first two STEM challenges in this book to teach the 4 C's, but also discuss what good collaboration looks and sounds like throughout the year. Periodically join any team that seems to struggle and ask questions until they see for themselves that they may be struggling with collaboration, then come up with ideas of how to improve that aspect of their team. The STEM introductory lesson of Paper Chains focuses on collaboration and how it helps the team build the longest strongest chain.

There are things you can do to foster collaboration even further than teamwork naturally will. First, make sure the teams are of mixed ability, diversity, and social capability. If a team is too small there may not be enough ideas evoked during brainstorming or redesigning, but if they are too large the shyer quiet individuals get left out. Teams of five are too big for STEM challenges and teams of two is often too small. Remind teams that nonparticipation is not an option. Call the timekeeper the time manager, so that they get their hands on things besides a clock. Remind teams that engineering is too difficult to do by yourself and that its complexity calls for too many parts for the process to be done alone.

Have collaboration check-ins and ask if all team members have had input. Find out if all team members feel heard. Ask if there is a division of labor. Remind students to have eye contact and listen just as much as they talk if not more. Ask teams not to make assumptions, but rather to ask clarifying questions. Ask students if they have an open mind and a positive attitude and if their actions and words can prove that. Remember as a team, you are not just taking up the same space physically in one spot in the room, but you should also be sharing the same thought process and decision-making.

Creativity

Creativity may be the most difficult thinking skill to teach, but is probably the most wanted in groups and in the workforce. It starts with imagination. Bloom says that creativity is the highest order thinking skill because it combines all the others. Creativity relies on being open to new ideas, employing divergent thinking, and maintaining a sense of flexibility. Creativity begins in the STEM challenge during the brainstorming of ideas for problem solutions. It is also needed in the step labeled "Imagine" which appears in many models. It is also the base word for the step of "Create" because putting an abstract plan together into a concrete format is a big leap.

Children enter school filled with curiosity, imagination, and wired for creativity. Too often over time that changes as many education systems only validate the "right" answer. To conform to expectations, these once creative children develop ways of thinking that actually hinder creativity. To think outside of the box is hard for students who have been taught to conform. Standardized tests that value only one right answer foster systems that do not value the alternative methods. Therefore, STEM is one way to provide a safe place for kids to be creative and relearn how to be creative.

Creativity is not just random and crazy thoughts, but rather a new way of looking at something and making it work differently and often in a better way. This is exactly what the redesign step in the engineering process is. In STEM challenges, it is important not to show students a prototype before they begin making their own. This will foster creating new and different solutions, not just the "right" one. Creativity can be present both in the product and in the process. Brainstorming is the time for the random and crazy thoughts, but staying on the task at hand is the job of the CEO. They can say something like, "That sounds like an outstanding idea, but look at the material we have to use."

Creativity is the ability to discover new and original ideas, connections, and solutions to problems. To navigate life successfully it takes ingenuity and finding shortcuts or workarounds, so everyone has creativity to some extent, some just seem to have more than others. People that are open to new experiences and willing to fail because it is a part of growing, become more creative. Again, this is what a STEM challenge is all about. Testing their designs to the failure point in order to make it better the next time, until that one fails and there is a new opportunity to get even better and so on. The more STEM challenges and the more iterations students participate in the more creative they become. Maya Angelou said, "You can't use up creativity. The more you use it, the more you have." You will probably find, as I have, that more students get more creative as the year goes on if you do STEM challenges often.

Creative people do not just sit around passively waiting for inspiration. They are playful and feel free to experiment. You as the teacher need to model your appreciation of creativity and show that you believe there is always more than one "right" answer and that there is definitely more than one right way to find an answer. During the discussion time ask students to share some of the crazy ideas that came up during the brainstorming period and ask teams to nominate the MCP, or most creative player.

Creative people tend to possess a great deal of both physical and mental energy. However, they also spend a lot of time quietly thinking and reflecting. During a STEM challenge there needs to be both a time for thinking and a time for action. Sometimes you may want to introduce the problem a day before starting a STEM challenge to allow some percolation time. Sometimes creativity needs an incubation period. Allowing space to move into groups, space to construct prototypes, and space to test will allow an outlet for the physical and mental energy. You as the teacher should end each STEM time with reflection discourse and it is during that time when the class will learn of the creativity that was used on different teams to solve the same problem.

Use the first two STEM challenges in this book to teach the 4 C's, but also discuss what creativity looks and sounds like throughout the year. The introductory lesson of Paper Chains focuses on creativity and how it helps a team solve a problem together.

You can nurture and grow creativity by having check-ins during the STEM activity. Remind teams that failure is just a door to the next opportunity. Some things to say to foster creativity: Rethink the last failure and don't ask "Why me?"; instead, ask "Why did that happen?"

- Way to take risks!
- Way to be open-minded.
- Way to think outside the box!
- Stress is a creativity killer-everyone take two deep breaths and begin again.
- We need some more creative juices flowing—everyone stop and jog in place for one minute.
- Be kind to yourself and stop over-thinking and being critical or judgmental of yourself for having crazy ideas.
- Some of the best ideas sounded crazy at first. Embrace crazy ideas.
- Weirdness is a good thing when trying to be inventive.
- That was very innovative!
- Creativity can also be about the process more than the end product.

Communication

The third "C" I want to communicate is communication, see what I did there? Communication is essential for the collaboration part of STEM. In order for students to work together they must be able to talk to one another. There are definitely ways to communicate without saying a word and that needs to be explained as well. Accountable Talk is a type of talk that moves learning forward by being accountable to the learning community, the accuracy of information, and rigorous thinking. Students hold themselves responsible for getting the facts right, for thinking through challenges together, and for following rules that encourage participation. Again, the CEO is ultimately in charge of getting their team back on track if they happen to derail.

Students can learn reasoning skills by talking and constructively arguing their way through problems to conclusions and solutions. Students can learn to think out loud. Group members have a shared responsibility to support one another and make sure all group members understand the problem of the challenge or the focus of the discussion.

Another step of the engineering design loop where communication is important and skills improve is the discussion that should happen after the first test and group members need to help one another accept failure and figure out how to fix the new problems and design flaws. Helping others in the group to understand involves paraphrasing, re-phrasing, using examples, active listening and building upon the contributions of others. That is why iterations are important. Building the tower or bridge or whatever over and over will require more collaboration, communication and creativity.

You may already have Accountable Talk posters around your classroom. Sample ground rules for group communication can be posted.

We will…

- Look at the speaker to show we are listening.
- Use facial expression and body language to show we are actively listening.
- Contribute at least one idea to the group discussion.
- Ask at least one question during the group discussion.
- Build upon what group members say.
- Ask clarifying questions if confused.
- Use polite ways to challenge speakers with whom we do not agree.
- Keep the volume appropriate so all in the group can hear, but other groups are not disrupted.

Depending on the age and experience of your students, you may need to post some Accountable Talk stems to help them articulate their ideas. Students will improve with practice and not require the stems, but it is a good way to give reluctant speakers a voice because it is very important for collaboration that every voice is heard.

Here are some sample stems if you do not have your own:

- I did not understand what you meant by …
- Can you explain…?
- I agree because …
- I disagree because …
- I like what you said about _____ because…
- To add on what you shared, what about …
- I want to piggyback on what _____ said with this…

Use the first two STEM challenges in this book to teach the 4 C's, but also discuss what good communication looks and sounds like throughout the year. For example, yelling and blaming are poor communication and will not be tolerated. Using the correct math and science terms may be important to communicate, but only if they are understood at each student's level. The Paper Chain activity in the introductory lesson will focus on communication and how to discuss a STEM challenge within a team.

Move around the room during STEM time and address each team based on their unique needs at the time instead of addressing the entire group from the front of the room. You will find that close proximity will encourage more questions. The classroom should always be an environment that is safe to express ideas and feelings not just on teamwork days. Build confidence with kind words and actions.

Things you can say to foster better communication are:

- Way to use positive feedback for your team!
- Show gratitude and appreciation for a teammate's idea or hard work.
- Listening is just as important for good communication as talking.
- Don't just say, "Good job" be specific and say things like, "That was a great idea or that was just what our team needed."
- Remember your body language is communicating to your team as well as your words. Fix your face and your posture to show your interest in the task at hand.
- Think of how you can reword a concern without blaming others.
- I love how this team is communicating with each other.
- Ask team members to clarify that idea more fully if you are confused.
- How can you disagree with someone in a respectful manner?

Critical Thinking

The final "C" is critical thinking. One definition of critical thinking is the ability to think clearly and rationally, understanding the logical connection between ideas. I would add that it is also questioning everything and not just accepting things at face value in order to find the best solution or conclusion given the present circumstances. The analysis step in the design process that follows testing a prototype is one example of using critical thinking in STEM. That is when students make the science and math connections to improve their design. That is when they are searching for the answer to, "Why did that happen?" and "Can we do better?"

Critical thinkers can:

- Understand the connection between ideas.
- Determine the importance and relevance of arguments and ideas.
- Recognize, build and evaluate arguments.
- Identify inconsistencies and errors.

- Approach problems in a consistent and systematic way without emotion.
- Reflect on their actions and conclusions.

Barry Beyer says it best, "Critical thinkers are skeptical, open-minded, value fair-mindedness, respect evidence and reasoning, respect clarity and precision, look at different points of view, and will change positions when reason leads them to do so." This is practiced extensively throughout a STEM challenge. Critical thinking would be a great life skill to teach as our students enter the information age they need to be equipped with some radar and filters to make sense of it all.

Critical thinking occurs when a person analyzes, evaluates, and interprets information and then applies it to form a judgment. Look at the engineering process: Define a problem, Brainstorm and imagine possible solutions, Plan and design a solution, Build a prototype, Test it and Analyze the results, Reflect to redefine the problem with the prototype and start through the process again. Do you notice the similarities? The engineering design process applies critical thinking and creative thinking at the same time.

Critical thinkers are self-evaluators, problem solvers, open-minded, good listeners, and eager to take on challenges. A critical thinker is someone who thinks actively and interacts constantly with the world. Critical thinkers are created and strengthened through STEM challenges. Every time something is added or taken away from the original idea and tested it causes the critical thinker to make sense of it all. It happens in an instant and continuously. During the sharing of ideas, you should highlight that when a team fixed a problem they practiced critical thinking. They will often still be thinking of ways they could have made their designs better. It is hard to turn off that thinking once you get it started. What a great problem to have.

Critical thinkers ask questions all the time and students must become critical thinkers in order to become independent learners that can problem-solve and think on their feet. This is exactly what a STEM challenge requires in order to be accomplished. Throughout the STEM challenge you can have a critical thinking check-in by saying one of the following:

- Ask your team if the last contribution was logical?
- Is there a connection between your structure and one in the real world?
- What did you just discover by adding the last component?
- You may not just disagree, you must be able to explain why you disagree.
- Analyze the problems you are having right now and think for a minute of how to get past this issue.
- Are there any other alternative solutions? Can you give an example before changing anything?
- What can we learn from this problem?
- What math concepts are at work here?
- What science concepts are at work here?
- What caused the problem with the first attempt? What are you focusing on with the second or third attempt?
- Can you make your process better?

Use the first two STEM challenges in this book to teach the 4 C's, but also discuss what critical thinking looks and sounds like throughout the year. Teach the 4 C's explicitly with the first two STEM challenges that follow, the paper chain and pipe cleaner challenges. The first introductory lesson is Paper Chains and focuses on teaching the teams skills of communication, collaboration, creativity, and critical thinking. Good luck and have fun.

Chapter 4
Hands-On Activities to Teach the Engineering Loop and the 4 C's

Paper Chains Challenge

This is the activity that is used to teach the 4 C's of STEM team skills in action. You are looking for creativity while students are doing the task to take note of and highlight after the challenge during the discourse. Also look for examples of good collaboration, communication, and critical thinking.

Materials: 2 pieces of paper (notebook, copy, construction, whatever is available), 12 inches masking tape, ruler, scissors—per group

*Teacher tip: put the strip of masking tape down the side of a twelve-inch ruler with a little hanging off the edge so teams can rip it off as needed. OR give younger students 12 separate one inch strips of masking tape due to their limited dexterity with tape in the first place.

No one gets extra materials because that is one of the constraints.

Do not show them any prototypes; just make sure they understand how to loop strips of paper together to form a chain. That is to glue the ends of one strip together forming a circle and then the next strip must be inserted through that loop before gluing its ends together.

Do not tell them to cut the paper vertically, or horizontally. That is for the team to decide.

Do not tell them to use the ruler or scissors, just make them available. All of this is the group's decision.

Divide the team into groups and give the materials to each group and state the **Problem:**

The **problem** is that there is a limited amount of paper and tape and we need to make as many paper chains as possible to decorate the room. Therefore, the challenge is to build the longest paper chain with only 2 pieces of paper and 12 inches of tape. If there is a tie, the strongest one will win.

Imagine where you have seen chains before and how they looked. For example necklaces, bike chains, or chain links.

Plan/ Design for a few minutes because you only have ten minutes total. (Demonstrate how to connect links.) Tape the ends of one paper strip together to form a circle or loop. Then stick one end of the next strip through that loop before taping it to its other end to make the new loop that is interlocked. Your chain is now two loops long.

It is time for the next step of the design process which is to **Create** the paper chain, **"Go!"**

Stop the activity when you see teams halfway done with their available tape. Have them lay their chains on the table and look at the progress of each group. Discuss what the strengths and weaknesses are of their chain compared to others and praise for good team **collaboration** by pointing out teams that had all members engaged and contributing ideas. Praise teams for examples of good **communication** by pointing out people that had cheerleaders or those that talked and agreed on the procedure before actually cutting paper or tape. Did any group assign jobs? Was one person in charge of cutting paper? How was the tape used? How was taping the pieces together accomplished? Give teams five more minutes to finish their chains.

Test the chains when time is up. Have one member from each group stand along the wall holding one end of their chain. Teams should stand several feet from each other and have another team member take the other end of the chain and walk toward the middle of the room as far as the chain will allow. They can lay it on the floor to measure, especially if that is a math skill you would like to reinforce, but it will probably be evident which is the longest. If there is a tie, the teacher will gently pull the chains, one end in each hand until one breaks.

For **critical thinking**, have a discussion of how each team worked through problems. Discuss the changes that were made after time was called the first time and comparisons were made. Discuss the changes made when the materials were running low. Highlight any **creative** ideas that emerged by looking at each chain's construction. Did they cut the paper along the long side or short side? Ask teams about their process and compare which led to speed or strength and which groups had fun or got frustrated. Let each group get back together for further analysis and discuss how they will make their next chain even longer.

Save the chains so the teams can compare and contrast their first and second chains. Repeat the activity with the same teams and same directions, except this time you do not need a halftime discussion. Another iteration can be done with three pieces of any color construction paper and the entire time of fifteen minutes for construction without stopping until test time. Test in the same manner to find the longest paper chain.

You may wish to review the design process with this task even though that will be done with the next challenge. Ask students what they think is the first step of a STEM challenge. Hopefully, they will say that it is becoming familiar with the problem. Write it on the board and draw an arrow to the next step and see if anyone can name the Imagine step. Write it on the board and draw an arrow. Ask what they do next and tell them to call that planning step, Design and write it on the board with another arrow. Sometimes that step requires a drawing and always requires a discussion before building the prototype or solution to the problem.

Write Create on the board and draw an arrow. Ask what the last step is and see if they can name it as Test and write it on the board. Testing a prototype means measuring its length, height, strength, or something. Then teams figure out what they need to fix on their own design through critical thinking like analysis, so draw an arrow back to plan and show that it is a process.

Another paper chain activity if time allows.

Problem: is not enough supplies. 3 pieces of construction paper and 12 inches of masking tape for each team to make the longest chain in 15 minutes

Imagine: what patterns can be made with the colors the group has chosen for example, school or holiday colors.

Design: what the problem's solution will be with more paper, but the same amount of tape and whether you are going to cut the paper lengthwise or widthwise.

Create: the chain, you have 15 minutes

Test: to see which team created the longest chain as well as if each team was able to get a longer chain. Did the extra paper help even though you had the same amount of tape?

Have a group discussion about what each team did differently and see if their chains were longer the second time, and why they think there were differences.

Communication, Collaboration, Creativity, and **Critical Thinking** are the 4 C's of STEM. Make a point of when each of the four occurred during the Paper Chain Challenge. Write the words on the board and discuss what each means as they relate to STEM.

What does good communication look like and sound like? Poor communication look and sound like? There are positive ways to say things. Instead of saying, "You are doing it all wrong!" Try to say, "It could be better if we did this, or that."

What does good collaboration look and sound like? Poor collaboration? If you see someone in your team sitting back and not feeling involved ask them what they want to do differently and to show you how that works. Ask someone to help you by holding this or that and smile more.

Who showed some creativity in this activity? How? For example, one team may have everyone making loops with half of the strips and then with the other half looping the circle links together. Other teams may be looping on each end at the same time.

Tell them critical thinking includes any of the following: observation, analysis, interpretation, reflection, evaluation, inference, explanation, problem-solving, and decision-making, and give examples from this activity. Ask one person to give an example of an observation they made during the challenge. Ask one person to reflect on what their team did differently the second time. Ask a different person to explain one problem their team had and what they did to overcome it. Point out the teams that cut the strips horizontally that would make the strips twelve inches long and the loops longer compared to teams that cut the strips vertically from the paper making the strips eight and a half inches long. How did the chain link lengths affect the overall length of the chain and its strength?

Ask each team how decisions were made, if they ran out of materials what did they do? Did the teams change their procedures after the half time was called?

Ask the longest chain team what they observed as the winning process. Use the chains to decorate the room.

Pipe Cleaner Tower Challenge

This challenge is also an introductory lesson. This challenge is designed to introduce the engineering design process and can also review the 4 C's. Write the loop on the board or show a premade poster that illustrates the engineering design process, **Problem-> Imagine-> Design-> Create-> Test->Improve** (draw an arrow that loops back to the design step because that is what gets repeated, design, create, test, design, create, test as long as time and materials allow.) Announce each step and point to it on the board or poster before reading aloud the parts the students need to know and identify it as the next step, or how it logically follows the previous step. If you use a premade poster that uses different wording, explain those steps that are synonymous for example, the design step is sometimes called the planning step.

Materials: **15 pipe-cleaners**

Problem: Our problem is that the United States no longer has the tallest tower in the world. We need some innovative engineers to design one that is. Every tower starts with a prototype, a small version to plan, display, and explain. Your challenge is to build this prototype of the tallest freestanding tower with only **15 pipe-cleaners** per group.

Group students into teams of 3-4.

*Teacher tip: younger students may need the pipe-cleaners cut in half prior to building. Remind students that the ends of pipe-cleaners have sharp metal prongs sticking out and to be careful. Define freestanding since the prototype needs to be able to represent a real tower. Freestanding means the structure cannot be held, taped, wedged between desks, etc.

Day 1

This activity will review the skills that help teams do STEM challenges more successfully as well as introduce the engineering loop.

Ask students to repeat **The Problem** in their own words. It is to build the tallest freestanding tower with only 15 pipe-cleaners.

Imagine other towers in the real world. What shapes are used and how is height increased? You can even show videos like the tallest towers in the world or read a book aloud about towers.

Design/ Plan: Every student must **creatively** draw his or her plan on a piece of paper first. This is different than the paper chain challenge when the group only had to talk before cutting the paper or tape. This time each member must draw a design they think would be best for height. This illustrates the creativity skill. After working for 5 minutes, stop and for the next five minutes have students **communicate** their design with their group. The group should decide on one plan, but it can combine any and/or all the ideas of each member.

Create: They should begin construction now that they have **collaborated** on a plan they must also work together on the actual construction. Remind them that they need to be good communicators and working together is called collaboration. After 5-10 minutes, stop the building and have them look around.

Analyze with **critical thinking** as a team what is going well, what is becoming frustrating, and how can other designs from the real world or the other groups help with their own design?

Allow them 5-10 minutes to finish. You may need a countdown if they are super engaged or the towers keep falling when not supported.

Announce, "Hands off" when time is up. Look around and see if teams are successful or if they need more time because materials was the intended constraint and time for construction always depends on the age and experience of the students as well as the variable of class schedules.

Test: Measure each tower either at the separate construction sites or in the center of the room at a "testing station". Measure in inches or centimeters or both with zero at the base. Hold the measuring tape or yardstick straight up vertically not leaning as the tower probably does. A string can be used to stretch from the apex of the tower tip horizontally to the number scale on the measuring device, or you can just eyeball it. Save towers to compare after day two.

Discuss the engineering loop: Problem-> Imagine-> Design-> Create-> Test->Analyze. Tell them they will improve their towers next. You decide if you have time and want to do the Day 2 directions now or on a separate day.

Ask how they did as engineers with the loop and what they did for each step with this activity. Review what the problem was and ask a student to restate it. What did they do for the Imagine step? What was done for the design step? Who can explain the create step? Who can explain the test step? When did your team analyze? Once they realize they did all the steps then congratulate them on being engineers!

Review the 4 C's: Who had great communication? Explain why that is a good example. Who had great collaboration? Explain why that is a good example. Who can give an example of creativity in this activity? How? Who can give an example of critical thinking which could include observation, analysis, interpretation, reflection, evaluation, inference, explanation, problem-solving, and decision-making, and give examples from this activity.

Day 2 can be run exactly as the first or you can try a variation. The teams stay the same, the materials stay the same, and the process stays the same. This activity is to teach the engineering loop. It can also be used on day 2 to review STEM team skills.

ETS1.C.1-Analyze data from tests of two objects designed to solve the same problem to compare the strengths and weaknesses of how each performs. This is the objective I use for this activity because there are two towers to compare. But any time the class builds the same end product you can compare the prototypes of each team to achieve this objective as well.

I will explain all the objectives that deal with engineering a little later in this chapter.

Pipe Cleaner Tower Challenge Variation for Day 2 or 3

Announce each step of the engineering loop:

Problem: The United States no longer has the tallest tower in the world. We need some innovative engineers to design one that is. Every tower starts with a prototype, a small version to plan, display, and explain. Your challenge is to build this prototype of the tallest freestanding tower with only 15 pipe-cleaners.

Get teams back together from the first tower challenge. Pass out bundles of 15 pipe-cleaners to each group. Have someone restate the problem as you pass out the pipe-cleaners, or as the material retriever in each group goes to the supplies table to count out 15 pipe-cleaners themselves. Remind the students that the engineering design process begins with a problem or a question and their challenge is to build the tallest freestanding tower.

Imagine: Think of real-world towers, such as The Eiffel Tower, Empire State, Liberty Memorial, <u>EVOLUTION of WORLD'S TALLEST BUILDING: Size Comparison (1901-2022)</u> (if you show this start at 23 seconds.) The imagine step is student engineers using their imagination to broaden their idea of what a tower is and how it could look. Reading a book aloud about towers is a great thing to do for younger students in the imagine step of the engineering design process.

Design: Draw or just have a group discussion because this is a day two and they have drawn it before, but now they have been shown real-world towers and may want to draw again. Their discussion could lead to giving out job assignments to group members because certain teammates may have had more success at certain jobs the first time around. After five minutes ask the students what step this was of the Engineering Process.

Create: When you say it is time to create, ask someone to tell you what that means they should be doing. Hopefully, they will answer that it is the building time. Say, "Go!" After working for 2-4 minutes: tell students to freeze. Say, "Your team had an unexpected budget cut, and one of your resources is gone. Each team member must now put one arm behind his/her back! Now continue."

2-4 more minutes later judging frustration levels have all students freeze again. Say, "Your engineering company sees that the loss in resources has hurt production. The manager has decided to expand your operations in order to bring in more business. Your team now does business in a foreign country and there is a language barrier. You may use both arms again, but now you do not speak the same language, so you must continue the task without speaking! Think of other ways you have learned to communicate and continue building the tower."

After another 1-2 minutes: Say, "Business is booming, and your company has hired translators. You can now complete the task with all your resources including talking! One minute left!"

Countdown from ten and stop the activity.

Test by measuring the height of each tower. Ask the students what it means to test a prototype. They should say that it is time to see if the teams solved the problem which this time it is to build the tallest freestanding tower.

Walk around the room and calling attention to the different shapes and designs of the towers. Determine the tallest tower and allow the team to explain their successful design and **Analyze** their process.

Teacher tip: adjust the time depending on how quickly students are working. Younger students may become paralyzed by the planning stage. Help them focus on building a sturdy foundation and may need pipe-cleaners cut in half. Some teams will ignore the rules that are imposed, so you may threaten to take away pipe-cleaners as a consequence!

The step not announced was **Analyze**, because that was the entire challenge do-over as well as the adjustments made by each team individually during construction, but point that out now. The problems that arise throughout construction kept making the loop start over because of the critical thinking, which is analyzing, that occurred simultaneously. The engineering loop evolves and happens without announcement. Students will see that in order to improve things engineers must go through a process and think about it as they go along. The final question is:

was the second tower an improvement over the first tower even with new problems introduced? Have teams set both towers side by side and compare and see if they improved.

ETS—Engineering, Technology, and Science Standards come from the Framework for K-12 Science Education from the NRC, National Research Council. They are referenced in the Next Generation Science Standards as one of their three pillars and taken from Common Core State Standards or CCSS that have been adopted verbatim by forty-two states and all the rest in some manner. The ETS standards have three main parts: A-defining an engineering problem. B-developing possible solutions. C-optimizing the design solution.

In the kindergarten through second grade band, there are three standards. The first one states the expectation that students will be able to ask questions, make observations, and gather information about a situation people want to change to define a simple problem that can be solved through the development of a new or improved object or tool. The second standard states that students will develop a simple sketch, drawing, or physical model to illustrate how the shape of an object helps it function as needed to solve a given problem. The third states students should analyze data from tests of two objects designed to solve the same problem to compare the strengths and weaknesses of how each performs.

What does this mean? It means that engineering should begin in kindergarten and that by the end of second grade students will understand that engineering challenges are asking them to develop a new or better object that will solve a problem. They should be able to either draw a picture or build a model that has a shape and/or function to solve that problem. Finally, they can compare their and others' models to see strengths and weaknesses. Each challenge I give can be simplified to these three expectations through the design process to the best of their ability.

At the next level, third through fifth grade students who demonstrate understanding can:

3-5-ETS1-1. Define a simple design problem reflecting a need or a want that includes specified criteria for success and constraints on materials, time, or cost.
3-5-ETS1-2. Generate and compare multiple possible solutions to a problem based on how well each is likely to meet the criteria and constraints of the problem.
3-5-ETS1-3. Plan and carry out fair tests in which variables are controlled and failure points are considered to identify aspects of a model or prototype that can be improved.

What does this mean? If your students have had STEM experiences in the earlier grades, you build on that and if not you have to begin simple before getting more complex. The problem step now includes criteria and constraints "delimiting" it, which often limits resources or time. There should be either iterations to compare or at the very least multiple solutions from all the teams to judge how well each team met the criteria and constraints. Finally, the testing of the models should control one aspect at a time in a fair way and can expect a point of failure in order to improve the prototype. Each challenge in this book hits all three standards if the engineering design process is followed.

Middle-school grades 6-8 build on the K-5 experiences and progresses to finding relationships between variables to clarify arguments and revise models to predict input and outputs. The data analysis progresses to finding correlation and causation to explain solutions in the natural and designed world. The challenges in this book lend themselves to gathering data if students have that skill and can be adapted in difficulty for students up to eighth grade.

Chapter 5
STEM Challenge Categories

You understand the roadblocks, you have a growth mindset, and you found that your students loved the introductory lessons. You like the design process and your students are collaborating and showing more creativity and critical thinking. Your introductory lessons were each done all on one day, but the rest of the challenges can be divided into five ten-minute chunks or done all at once, whichever fits your schedule best. Keep that momentum going with nine more months of STEM challenges! You started with a pipe cleaner tower challenge and we will keep that going with variations on tower-building. There are also chapters on cars, catapults, boats, bridges, mazes, houses, planes, and solar cookers to create, test and redesign. Let the fun begin!

Each category will begin with some background information and explain some of the science and math skills involved in the challenge. The background may also include history and give examples of solutions to real-world problems that engineering has solved. You may choose to read the background information aloud to the student in part or in its entirety. You may choose to have students research beyond what I provide, but it is not necessary.

There are books that would be a great way to introduce each category as well. I love reading a short book aloud about towers before building a single tower. I chose to limit any book suggestions because that is a personal decision based on the age and ability of the students. I do believe you can read books aloud that are above the students' ability because you are doing the reading and thinking aloud. I also believe that older students can enjoy picture books and easy readers for specific introductory purposes. Teachers that use oral reading in the classroom will feel comfortable with this idea and teachers that do not will not. I suggest finding a book with a ton of pictures and reading it aloud to introduce the idea of cars before building any cars. There are many books on many reading ability levels about boats and bridges, etc. I believe even older students enjoy being read to. I know younger students can be shown detailed and complex schematics and listen to readings above their grade level comprehension.

There are also many books about engineering itself that can be read aloud. I know there are things on the internet tied to books and could have given you suggestions for each category, but did not want you to feel that you had to go out and purchase anything special. Go to the library and find some to check out. The ones for engineering in general can be found in your local library if not in your school library. I read *Rosie Revere Engineer* by Andrea Beatty to every age level, kindergarten through 8th grade, to introduce engineering and the idea of persistence. I also have read her other books *Iggy Peck Architect* and *Ada Twist Scientist* for examples of other characteristics needed in the pursuit of STEM.

I also suggest not showing any prototype models prior to doing any STEM challenge. Too many students will feel there is only one right way to solve a problem and try to replicate the model you show them. This often cramps the creativity of the students. If your students lack experience with things in the challenges such as a truss bridge you can use internet searches to see examples of real cars and bridges and catapults, but I would not look at kid-made. You will find some internet resources mentioned in the challenges that I have found useful to view before starting a challenge build especially at the **Imagine** step. Students need to struggle with seeing the potential and limitations of the materials they have available and feel free to explore. Students need to feel comfortable taking risks and not being discouraged with failure.

Towers

Towers are fun and a great way to get students measuring. Kids begin building towers when they are babies with blocks and get more sophisticated with age, experience, and materials. You can read this background information about towers aloud or just read it yourself and paraphrase.

One real-world problem associated with towers is real estate. As cities ran out of room architects built up instead of out. Architecture is the science of designing buildings. Architects use math and science to create designs called blueprints that tell them how to build things like houses, schools, and office buildings. Before they start building, architects will do tests to check that the materials they are using are strong and safe. All of these ideas can be incorporated into STEM challenges.

Towers have been built in all shapes and sizes and for multiple purposes over the centuries, but the ongoing construction challenge with tower-building is for teams to design and build towers taller while still remaining stable. Teams must figure out how to get their tower to go up without toppling over. Older students would benefit from a discussion of the forces acting on the tower, such as gravity. Each new tower you will introduce new material, but the challenge with tower-building still remains, "How high can we build it?" Provide rulers, measuring tapes, and meter sticks. Show the students how to measure from the base up in different units.

Building a tower is a battle with gravity versus the building materials. A discussion of how to best use those materials should include how to make the tower stronger and also balance them carefully so each part of the tower supports the other. Gravity is that invisible force that is constantly pulling objects toward the center of our planet.

In general, a wider base makes a more stable tower. Perhaps revisiting the pipe cleaner challenge will elicit that there were certain geometric shapes that were better than others, like triangles. Many world famous towers illustrate how a wide base relative to its height makes it very stable, for example The Eiffel Tower. There is a ratio of its width to its height that works best. That is a complex math concept you can do with older students while tower-building.

There are many reasons towers are built. Towers have solved many real-world problems, which is the first step of the engineering design process. Towers let you see a long distance which is good for things like a fire watch and lookouts for bad weather or approaching enemies. Towers also can be seen from a long distance away like lighthouses that help ships avoid rocky shores. Towers are easily defensible from attack; if you can imagine castles and the Great Wall of China, you get the idea of how towers were used for this in the past. Towers are a compact way to store things like grains in silos. Towers allow a lot of people to live and work in a smaller area because apartment buildings and skyscrapers are also an example of towers. Many towers are pretty and good for landmarks, there is the Leaning Tower of Pisa, the Chrysler Building in New York City, and the Empire State Building also in New York, just to name a few.

You can present any tower challenge as solving one of these problems. You can run towers as all teams building with the same materials or the challenge of building with any two materials that teams find available. I have even had tower stations using several different materials and material combinations. To explore tower-building, I had stations around the room with materials spread out on table tops. I had twenty-eight students so I had seven stations and four students on each team. You can add more if you prefer three man teams or subtract a station if you have fewer students. I am just explaining my process.

There was one area with dominoes, another station with Jenga blocks, one with plastic cups, one with Legos, one with Lincoln Logs, one with K-nex, and one with magnetic geometric blocks. You can use whatever material you have available. Each area had its own meter stick and a paper to record the tallest height reached with just that material by each team. I blew a whistle every ten minutes that meant to measure and record before rotating to the next station. After almost two hours each team had built several different towers using different building material, measured seven different towers, and recorded their best attempts. The reflection discussion that followed analyzed each team's experience and elicited what was successful as well as what was not.

You may not have any of those materials, and prefer to purchase some inexpensive building material. Most tower construction is best with two different types of material, one that is long for the building sections such as, uncooked spaghetti, toothpicks, skewers, straws, etc. The other material for tower construction is for connecting the sections, such as miniature marshmallows, playdough, clay, tape, etc. Some examples for tower material combinations are: uncooked spaghetti and miniature marshmallows, toothpicks and playdough, or stick pretzels and large marshmallows, or drinking straws and tape, or skewers and gumdrops, or pencils and clay. You can spend your first month building towers or revisit them seasonally.

Example:

STEM Challenge—Spaghetti Towers

A sample of an 'I Can' statement for those of you required to post those would be: I can build the tallest freestanding tower out of uncooked spaghetti and miniature marshmallows.

A sample of the standards covered by most engineering challenges (remember this is the wording for the grades 3-5 band):

ETS1-1. Define a simple design problem reflecting a need or a want that includes specified criteria for success and constraints on materials, time, or cost.

ETS1-2. Generate and compare multiple possible solutions to a problem based on how well each is likely to meet the criteria and constraints of the problem.

ETS1-3. Plan and carry out fair tests in which variables are controlled and failure points are considered to identify aspects of a model or prototype that can be improved.

Materials: Each group gets: 20 pieces of uncooked spaghetti, 20 miniature marshmallows, meter stick

Safety: Use meter sticks to measure only when everyone on the team is ready.

Do not put any spaghetti or marshmallows in your mouth as they are dirty and germy.

Problem: We need a prototype of a tower to use as a lookout

Imagine solutions by thinking of towers you have seen or built or read any of the background information that you believe will help.

Design: each team member draws a plan on white paper for a tower.

Share **plans** and note the good ideas of each to combine into a team endeavor.

Create: Build towers: Another constraint besides material is time. Planning takes time, construction takes time, and testing takes time, but it is always best if there is time for a redesign and retest for the tower to be analyzed by the team members.

Test: The tower must be freestanding and is measured from the base up. Freestanding means it cannot be held, lean on anything, or be taped to the base. Improvements were made throughout the process. This happened throughout construction each time a section was added and then was let go to see if it stayed upright. A final official measurement can be done by the teacher when time is up.

Analyze: Compare each tower and discuss strengths and weaknesses. This is the time to ask thought provoking questions. Examples are: What shapes do you see in most towers? Why is that shape a good one for towers? How does this challenge prove there is gravity? What was one good way to add extra height at the very end like many of the famous towers? (adding a steeple or spire, which is just one single spaghetti stuck up like an antenna) How did you measure your tower? What happened the first time you let go during construction and what did you do about it?

The next week can be spent doing an iteration of the spaghetti towers or try one of the following variations using different materials and introducing a different problem that can be solved by constructing a tower.

Variations for Towers

Variation 1: The **problem** is lack of space downtown and needing to design a new apartment building or office skyscraper. It is up to you if you want to add more criteria like most interesting looking to appeal to tenants or tallest again and I would definitely require them to be freestanding.

Materials can be toothpicks and playdough, or stick pretzels and large marshmallows, or drinking straws and tape, or skewers and gumdrops, or pencils and clay. Any long stable sticklike object and any connecting material to be the vertices can be used to build towers.

- Teacher tip: Some students may need to build cubes and pyramids to learn about three-dimensional properties prior to tower-building.

Go through the process, Imagine->Design->Create->Test->Analyze

Imagine other apartment buildings you have seen or lived in.
You have 5 minutes to **Design** by looking at the available materials and discuss or draw out your ideas for a group discussion with your team.
You have 10 minutes to **Create** your structure.
It is time to present your apartment building and explain the process used to design and create it. Allow the others to ask questions. The **Test** will be if it met the criteria that was chosen in your problem presentation, which is to be the tallest freestanding tower.
The **Analysis** is during the sharing of structures and I cannot script that for you as it depends on what transpired during construction time.

Tower Variation 2: The **Problem** is that ships cannot see the shallow areas and where the shoreline is irregular and unsafe, so you need to design a lighthouse prototype.

Materials can be 20 straws and a roll of masking tape or 20 pencils and ½ cup of clay or playdough.

Go through the process, Imagine->Design->Create->Test->Analyze

Imagine other lighthouses you have seen.
Draw your **design** on paper after looking at the material you will have for construction.
Create your lighthouse tower
Test to see which tower is the tallest that met the criteria of using only the given materials
Analyze the difficulties the new material presented and how the team overcame any problems during the create step.

Tower Variation 3: The question is who can create the most interesting holiday structure to display downtown during holiday times?

Materials: **gumdrops and toothpicks around holiday times when gumdrops are on sale**
Go through the process, Imagine->Design->Create->Test->Analyze

Problem: Can you create a holiday structure using only toothpicks and gumdrops to display during the holidays?

Imagine: What are some shapes you can you use to represent the holidays?

Design: Draw your ideas on paper to share with your team to come up with a collaborative decision.

Create: You have ten minutes to build your holiday structures

Test: Share your creations and explain your ideas, process, and what it is supposed to represent

Analyze: Compare and contrast the creations that all the teams presented

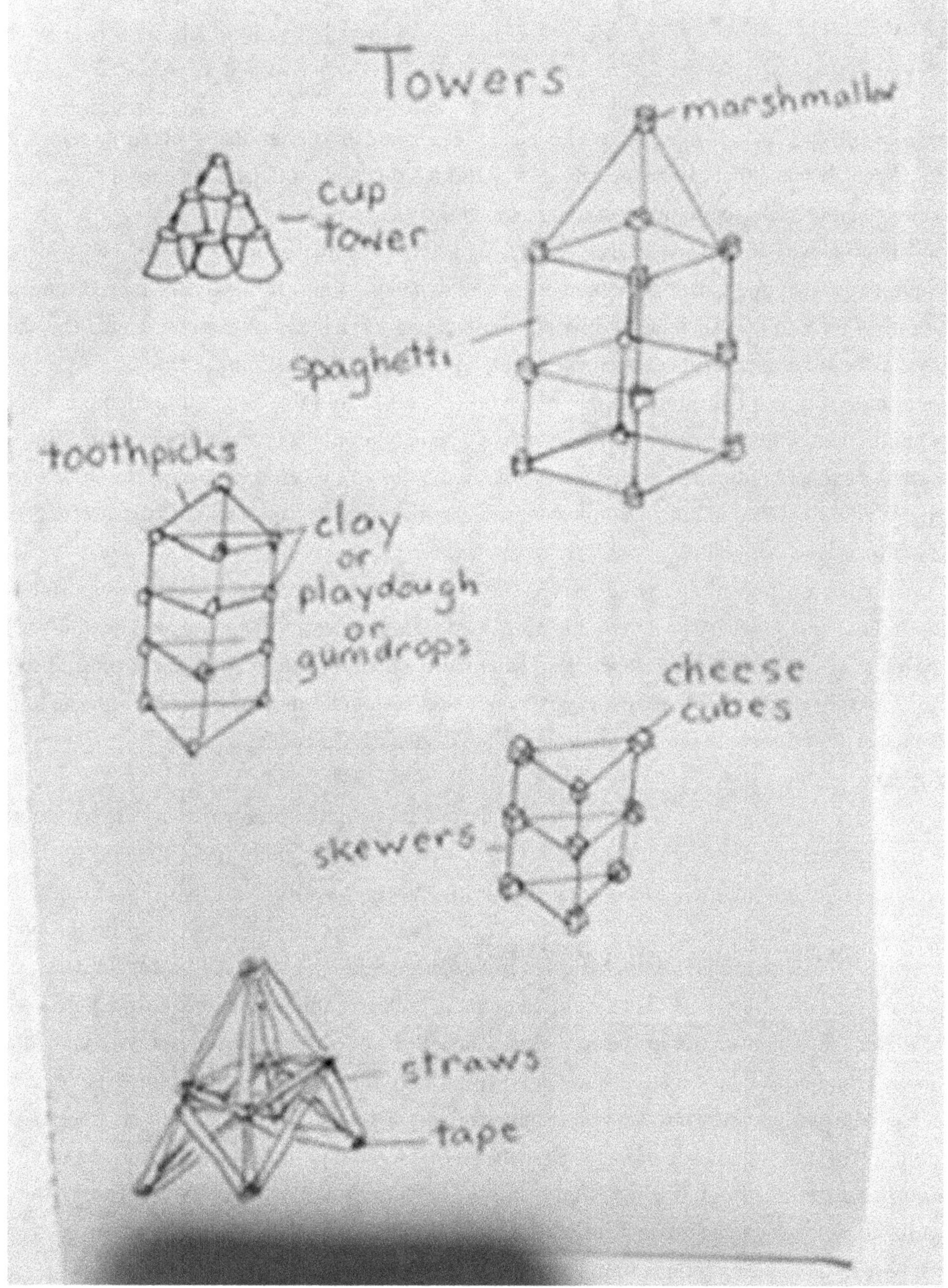

Chapter 6
Cars

Another category of STEM challenges is cars because there are many variations of creating cars. Cars are any vehicle that moves a distance that can be measured even though they may look and move more like a sled, we call them cars. Here is some background information or you could have students research for themselves.

Can you imagine why vehicles were invented? What was the real-world problem? People need to get themselves and loads from one place to another. As a way to carry goods efficiently for long distances, wheeled vehicles were invented and this allowed for broader trade networks. Instead of carrying goods themselves or on animals, farmers and other merchants created carts with wheels to do the carrying.

Transportation is a fun study of how people move things and people from one place to another and has been explored by children since they started playing with toys. I remember my son was still sitting in a highchair when he took his green bean and pretended it was a car as he made the vroom-vroom car noises and scooted it across the tray. A baby's first books and puzzles topics are often transportation vehicles like a bus, a firetruck, a car, a boat, and the little engine that could.

Sailing chariots, propelled by the wind, were used in China when Marco Polo visited in 1600. There are drawings throughout history that show real and imagined vehicles for moving people and things. Karl Benz patented the first true, modern automobile. He also patented his own throttle system, spark plugs, gear shifters, a water radiator, and other things used on cars. Henry Ford and his Model T met the demand for basic transportation on a larger scale in the 1920s with the assembly line. Today besides Mercedes Benz and Fords there are all types and brands of cars.

The gas combustion engine enabled the "horseless" carriage. The initial problem of how to move and transport things evolved into how to improve that process, so cars became smaller, more fuel-efficient, less polluting and safer. Products and their production was a process of solving ever arising problems by using computers in design, engineering, and the manufacturing to create even larger, faster, more stylish cars. Then the problems of fuel shortages gave rise to electric engines with batteries and other alternative sources of power for cars. A car design competition that uses only solar power is held for students in college engineering classes every year.

Cars are a great way to study force and motion because the work of overcoming gravity and friction to get something to move is fun. When you tell the students, you want them to invent a new prototype for a car you can decide what problem you want them to address. Some of their cars may have wheels; others may look more like sleds. The point is to get it to move. This usually means having a ramp to use gravity to start the motion, or a sail to use wind, or a rubber band to utilize potential energy. The body of the car itself will depend on the materials you have available. Chassis can be made from recyclable material like water bottles or juice boxes or paper towel tubes, Legos, K-nex, or as in the annual Soap Box Derby, blocks of wood.

In science, motion is the phenomenon in which an object changes its position with respect to time. To better understand how to get their vehicles to move students may need an introduction of the laws of motion or a few definitions. Force is a push or a pull. A push is a force that will cause an object to move forward faster or in a different direction. A pull is the force that slows a moving object down or makes it stop. Gravity pulls all objects down toward the earth.

Sir Isaac Newton formulated three laws of motion. The first is that every movement is a result of a force because objects at rest will stay at rest (because of gravity) unless an outside force acts on it. Also if an object is in a uniform motion it will stay in that motion until an outside force acts on it. Again, gravity and friction will cause their cars to slow down and stop eventually.

The second law explains that speed and direction is determined by force. In other words, the harder you push or throw, the faster or farther an object will move. The mass also plays a factor here because the lighter an object the less force is needed to make it move and vice versa the more mass the more force is needed.

The third law states that for every action there is an equal and opposite reaction. For example, when the air rushes out of the balloon attached to a car, the car is pushed the opposite direction, so have the balloon inflator tube facing the opposite direction you want the vehicle to move. Friction is the resistance of motion when one object rubs against another. Anytime two objects rub against each other, they cause friction. Friction works against the motion and acts in the opposite direction. Some friction is good or we would not be able to walk, just think about icy sidewalks or waxed floors when the friction is decreased and we can't get any traction. Look at the soles of shoes to see how friction is increased for sports and decreased for dancing.

In math, the idea of surface area needs to be related to friction. The more surface area of the car that comes into contact with the racetrack will increase the amount of friction there is, so less is more. The less surface area that comes into contact will increase distance or speed. The idea of wheels lifting the body of the car up off the ground is to decrease the amount of contact there is. If the wheels will roll, that would be an extra bonus in decreasing the friction because it decreases the rubbing of the two contact surfaces. Some axles don't rotate and that will increase the friction and at that point a team may ditch the wheels. A car is not defined by the presence of wheels.

Example: **STEM Challenge—Wind-Powered Cars**
I can build a wind-powered car that will travel the farthest

ETS1-1. Define a simple design problem reflecting a need or a want that includes specified criteria for success and constraints on materials, time, or cost.
ETS1-2. Generate and compare multiple possible solutions to a problem based on how well each is likely to meet the criteria and constraints of the problem.
ETS1-3. Plan and carry out fair tests in which variables are controlled and failure points are considered to identify aspects of a model or prototype that can be improved.

Materials: Each group gets: Recycled material such as, Cardboard Tubes (long and short), small cardboard boxes, cardboard pieces, wooden skewers or pencils (axles), pipe-cleaners, cardstock, construction paper, straws, masking tape (as much as needed) For the testing: Fan and meter stick.

Safety: Use meter sticks and fans only when everyone on the team is ready.
Keep the race track clear when testing vehicles.

Problem: Because of rising fuel prices and limited fossil fuels we need to explore alternative sources of energy. Design and build a prototype of a car that uses the wind for power to move the car the farthest
Imagine solutions by thinking of cars or other wind-powered vehicles like sailboats you have seen or built. What features help them capture wind?
Design: each team member draws a plan on white paper for a car.
Share **plans** and note the good ideas of each to combine into a team endeavor.
Create: Build Cars: Construct the body of the car with recycled material that is available. You should design it with aerodynamics in mind since wind is the power used for movement. That is the only constraint, so you may

or may not attach wheels with an axle, but should attach a sail or wings to capture enough wind. It will depend on time whether you have self-testing time to redesign before the entire class races or test the cars.

Test: Place the car at the starting line in front of the fan(s) and hold it there until given the "Go!" Turn off the fan(s) after a minute or two and measure how far the car traveled. You may have tape on the floor along the side of the raceway to mark every foot or yard or meter. You may need to teach students how to lay their ruler or meter stick end over end if the car travels very far and you do not have a measuring tape. Record the distance and repeat for each car. Students should observe how each car reacts with the wind in order to analyze the motion to **improve** the car for the next iteration.

Analyze: Compare each car and discuss the strengths and weaknesses of each. Discuss the construction experience of each team. What was one problem your team faced and how did you overcome it? Did you have wheels and how did that evolve? How was friction a factor in your car's movement? Did you have a sail or wings and what was the shape you chose for them and why? What would you differently next time?

Redesign and retest as often as time allows.

Variations for Cars

This entire car challenge can be redone using K-nex or Legos or even vegetables for the chassis of the car. Different materials make it a different STEM challenge.

Car Variation 1:

This car challenge can be redone without fans and sails where ramps are used instead and cars begin at the top and the force of gravity will get the car to move. The ramps can be built by elevating one end of a stiff, smooth plank so that it rests on a stack of books or blocks or even a small table or chair.

Present the **problem** of moving a load down a hill.

Imagine vehicles they have seen and ridden in. Read a book aloud with pictures of cars.

Allow time for them to **Plan** a **Design** and collaborate with their newly assigned team. It is up to you whether you wish to require a drawing or sketch of a proposed car design.

Using materials available allow time for the teams to **Create** their car. Again, it is up to you whether you want to use the same recyclable material for every team or allow any empty container as the chassis. Empty water bottles and paper towel tubes make great car chassis.

The **Test** is to measure how far the cars travel past the end of the ramp. You may need to add some types of weights that can be attached to the car in the materials list, such as small rocks, magnets, blocks, etc. because the cardboard and plastic chassis may not be heavy enough. Gravity and mass is at work and this is when the study of force becomes fun because there will be many "aha" moments. Other teams may have the idea to add wax paper or something to the ramp to decrease friction. That is up to you, but do not suggest it.

Analyze by asking thought provoking questions. I can't script it because of your unique experience, but I can tell you that you want to compare and contrast between teams and between first and second attempts by the same team.

Car Variation 2:

Another variation of the car challenge can be redone without fans or ramps. The energy could be from a rubber band attached to the body of the car and an axle that is wound up and then released. You would need to add **different size rubber bands and paper clips or other ways to attach the rubber band to the body and axle** to the materials list. Potential energy converting to kinetic energy is at work here. The question could be: Can you get a car to move without wind or gravity?

Go through the process, Problem or question->Imagine->Design->Create->Test->Analyze

Problem: There is no wind, there is no hill. How can we increase the potential energy of our car?

Imagine: Think about windup toys that you turn a knob or crank and when released it will hop or spin or move somehow

Design: Draw your ideas on paper of how to get a rubber band attached to a wheel's axle and the car to wind it up

Create: Your team has 10 minutes to build a rubber band powered car

Test: Wind your car up and measure how far it travels

Analyze: Compare and contrast the different types of ideas and process that were used in the car creations of different teams

Car Variation 3:

Thinking of potential energy and wind together an inflated balloon comes to mind. Attach a balloon to a straw and then attach the straw to the car body. Inflate the balloon and keep the air from escaping until race time. This is a different type of wind power. Add **balloons and straws** to the materials list.

Go through the process, Problem or question->Imagine->Design->Create->Test->Analyze

Problem: Can you use a balloon to move a car the farthest distance?

Imagine: What it looks like when air is blown into a balloon and then allowed to escape. Remember the law of motion that mentions the equal and opposite force and motion concepts.

Design: A balloon-powered car.

Create: Your team's balloon car.

Test: To see how far your car moves from the starting line when air is added and released on the word, "Go"

Analyze: Compare and contrast the different types of ideas and process that were used in the car creations of different teams.

There are kits you can purchase that use solar energy for small car designs. Solar energy is free, but the cells that capture the sunlight are not.

You can spend your second month of Fridays building and racing cars. Ready…Set… Go!

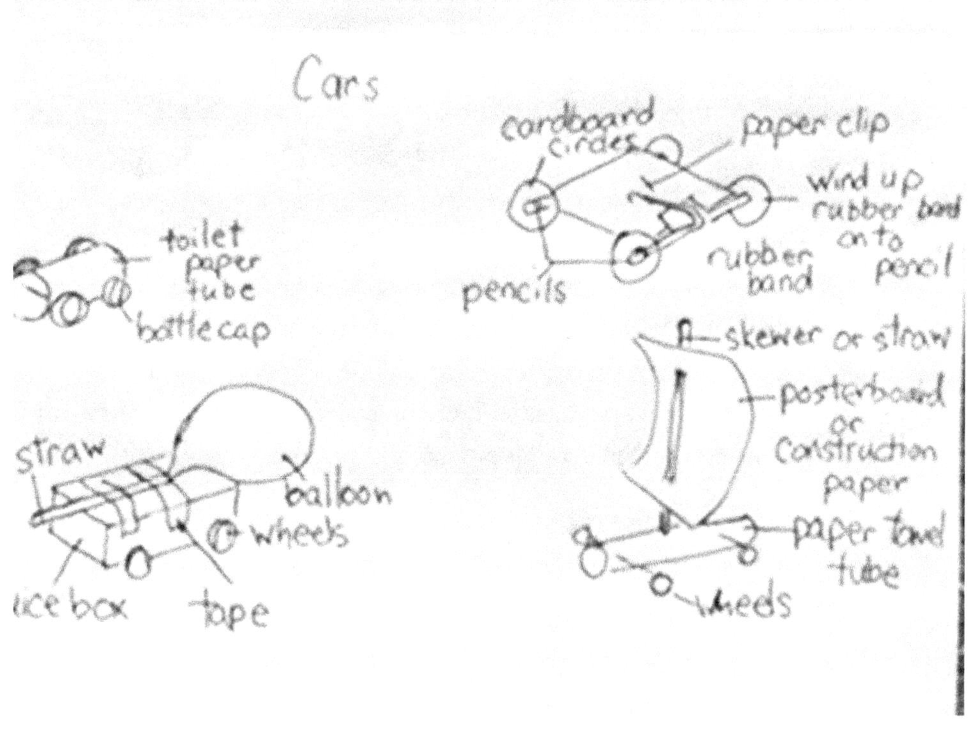

Chapter 7
Boats

Another category of STEM challenges that has many variations is boats. Hitchhiking on the transportation idea started with cars you can evolve into the study of boats. Boats are another type of transportation. Besides getting it to move faster or farther, you can set the problem as one of carrying the most cargo before sinking. It is messier and calls for having a room with a sink or some outdoor body of water so it is not for the faint of heart. You may choose to skip this category, but I assure you it is super fun. Water does spill, but it also dries rapidly. Here is some background information about boats or you may choose to research yourself.

Archimedes, a Greek scientist that lived over 2000 years ago, developed a scientific principle that would predict if something would float or not. Archimedes found out that buoyancy equals the weight of the liquid that an object displaces. If an object in water pushes aside an amount of water equal to the weight of the object (like a boat), it will float. If not, it will sink. Kids have been playing around with this idea ever since they started taking a bath as a toddler. Some bath toys float really well, some float for a while before sinking, and others never float at all. Even the ones that floated were fun to figure out a way to make them sink.

Water exerts an upward force upon objects called the buoyant force. When the downward force of gravity or weight of an object is greater than the water's buoyant force, the object sinks. When the weight is less, the object floats, and when equal, the object will remain at some level in the water. The greater the surface area of the object being placed in water, the more buoyant force it has applied to it to help it float. Density, or the amount of matter contained in a space also affects whether it will float. A small gold ring will sink, but the same size cork will float because gold is denser than cork.

Also, along this line even if it is the same material but packed into a smaller area, it is less buoyant. You can demonstrate this before the foil boat challenge by starting with two pieces of aluminum foil approximately nine to sixteen square inches in area. Leave one flat and wad one into a ball. Gently place both into a container of water and the ball if dense enough with float whereas the flat piece will float until water is splashed on top of it.

The real-world problem that needed to be solved was transporting people and goods across water. Boats are vehicles that float and move on or in water. Different types of boats solved different problems that evolved from that initial dilemma. The distance to cross, the power to move the boat, and the amount it could carry are some examples of problems that gave rise to different types of boats.

The science at work is buoyancy and the math concept to bring up is surface area and volume. When you laid the foil out flat in the water it had not only less density, but it also had more surface area. When teams shape the foil into elliptical and spherical shapes they are creating a three-dimensional object that not only has length and width, but also depth. The more volume a boat has the more passengers it will be able to carry. Bring this up during the discourse not prior to the challenge by questioning the students until they bring out that concept themselves.

Example: **STEM Challenge—Foil Boats**

I can build a boat from foil that will hold the most penny passengers

These standards are the K-2 grade band wording and are met when an engineering challenge goes through the design process.

ETS 1. Ask questions, make observations, and gather information about a situation people want to change to define a simple problem that can be solved through the development of a new or improved object or tool.

ETS 2. Develop a simple sketch, drawing, or physical model to illustrate how the shape of an object helps it function as needed to solve a given problem.

ETS 3. Analyze data from tests of two objects designed to solve the same problem to compare the strengths and weaknesses of how each performs.

Materials: Each group gets: a small tub of water, paper towels, aluminum foil, wax paper, tape, 10-20 pennies (marbles can be substituted). Having a beach towel for each group also keeps the mess to a minimum.

Safety: It is one person's job to add pennies one at a time. It is a different person's job to retrieve the sunken materials that must be dried before retesting.

Work with your team in a positive manner with cooperation and kindness.

Problem: We need to transport as many passengers as possible across a bay. Build a prototype of a boat that will float with the most passengers which will be represented by pennies.

Imagine solutions by thinking of boats you have seen or built

Design: each team member draws a plan on white paper for a boat.

Share **plans** and note the good ideas of each to combine into a team endeavor.

Create: Build Boats: Allow the material retriever to get as much foil, wax paper, and tape as needed for attempt one, but must not return for more until the boat has been tested and they can explain what they still need and why they believe that will help. The boat should be constructed with volume and square area in mind as well as remaining waterproof.

Test: The boat should be laid in the tub half full of water gently. The penny passengers should be placed into the boat one at a time keeping the center of gravity in mind (place them in the middle in concentric circles, in order not to tip the boat to one side, maybe allowing water to spill over). The passenger that made it sink does not count as the one before it was the maximum capacity before sinking. The boat that holds the most passengers is the winner if it is a friendly competition, but it is better if the team builds another boat that holds more passengers and competes with themselves to get a personal best so that everyone feels success.

Analyze: Compare each boat and discuss strengths and weaknesses. Ask questions about buoyancy. Ask about the shape of the boats. Ask about problems of sinking and floating and how they overcame it as a team. Review the skills of communication and collaboration and ask for examples from each team that saw good examples from teammates. Review creativity and critical thinking and ask for examples that each team saw of good examples from their teammates.

Variations for Boats

Boat Variation 1:

Change the boat construction materials and this becomes a new STEM lesson because of the properties of the new material. This STEM challenge can be redone when the boat is made of ¾ **cup of clay or playdough**. Remember to create new teams and go through the design process:

Problem->Imagine->Design->Create->Test->Analyze

Problem: What style of boat can carry the most penny passengers?

Imagine: Think about what you learned with the foil boat and shapes of other boats you have seen. Perhaps read a book about boats.

Design: Discuss with your team the process you want to follow and assign jobs to each team member

Create: You have 5 minutes to build your boat

Test: Place pennies in the boat until it sinks, make adjustments and test again. Record the amount of penny passengers for each attempt

Analyze: Bring your boat and data to the circle to discuss your process and results to see how each team solved the problem

Boat Variation 2:

The boat STEM challenge can be redone with any new boat construction material. The boat material can be **20 craft sticks and 12 inches duct tape.** The boat material can be varied by whatever is available and can be made to float. Plastic straws could work for parts of the construction, but are easily sunk if water gets inside of the straws, so there must be time to experiment.

Problem->Imagine->Design->Create->Test->Analyze

Problem: What style of boat can carry the most penny passengers with this new material?

Imagine: What type of boats are made of wood? What does a raft look like?

Design: Draw your ideas on paper and get together with your team to share and combine the best

Create: You have 10 minutes to build your boat

Test: Place pennies on the boat until it sinks, make adjustments and test again. Record the amount of penny passengers for each attempt

Analyze: Bring your boat and data to the circle to discuss your process and results to see how each team solved the problem

Boat Variation 3:

The boat can be made of **recycled or found materials** they bring from home such as water bottles or Styrofoam trays, but then attach a sail instead of counting passengers because the volume cannot be controlled because everyone will bring in different materials for the body of the boat. The race may need to be done in an outdoor fountain or creek or other body of water if a long tub or trough is not available, in order to get some distance to the race. If it is not windy, the teams can fold an accordion fan to create gusts of wind. The test would be to see which boat can reach the finish line the quickest. That means if there is only room for one boat at a time each race must be timed and the fastest time wins. During the analysis review creativity because these boats will be unique since there was not a constraint on the materials.

Problem->Imagine->Design->Create->Test->Analyze

Problem: The STEM challenge is to alternative energy sources, such as wind. Using recyclable material and wind energy who can get their boat to travel the farthest.

Imagine: Think about what you learned with the car challenge and sails for wind energy. Videos of a sailing regatta which is a series of sailboat races would be good to show. Background information could include stories about the America Cup or famous ships like the Mayflower or the Kon-Tiki or Ra II.

Design: Look through recycling bins to find items that could float and be adapted with sails and bring them in for the team to discuss and select.

Create: You have 10 minutes to build your boat

Test: Place the boat in the body of water and time how long it takes to get it to the finish line. If outside and windy that would be great, but wind can be simulated with an electric fan or accordion folded paper fan. Record the time.

Analyze: Bring your boat and data to the circle to discuss your process and results to see how each team solved the problem and which boat was the fastest. Redesign and retest as time allows.

Boat Variation 4:

Another type of boat that can be made of recycled or found materials is a pontoon style. This challenge can be either a race for a certain distance with an alternative power source or to hold the most weight before sinking. It is for older students and puts all the previous learning together. A pontoon boat has a flat deck that sits on top of 2 or three empty cylindrical tubes called pontoons. The engineering challenge is to find objects that float and then create a flat boat surface that will sit on top. One real-world problem is being marooned from a shipwreck and using the resources from an island to build a raft. In the Imagine step share pictures or stories about some famous boats like Kon-Tiki and Ra II. The Kon-Tiki proved in 1947 that a balsa wood raft could travel 5,000 miles of ocean from Peru to Polynesia in 101 days. The same man Thor Heyerdahl led a crew in 1970 to build another boat from papyrus (paper) and travel from Morocco across 4,000 miles across the Atlantic Ocean to Barbados in 57 days. He proved that ancient people could have travel farther than ever imagined before Ahoy there mates, you can spend your third month of Fridays engineering boats.

Problem->Imagine->Design->Create->Test->Analyze

Problem-> How can you design a pontoon boat that will carry the most weight?
Imagine-> Think of other famous boats and what they looked like and how they behave
Design->Look at the found materials and draw plans for your team's boat then collaborate to decide on one best use of ideas
Create-> You have 15 minutes to build your pontoon boat
Test->Bring your boat to the water to see how much weight it can hold
Analyze all the boats and see why the boat that held the most met that criteria

There are other solutions to the problem of transporting across bodies of water such as bridges. Along these lines in the next challenge category of bridge building the older students could also have a variation of building a pontoon bridge. A pontoon bridge, also known as a floating bridge, uses floats or pontoons to support a continuous deck for pedestrian and vehicle travel. The buoyancy of the supports limits the maximum load that they can carry and distance it is safe to cross. Most pontoon bridges are temporary and used in wartime and civil emergencies. Bridges is our next category to explore. Start simple with just paper and evolve to suspension with recyclable materials.

Boats

forces of gravity and density

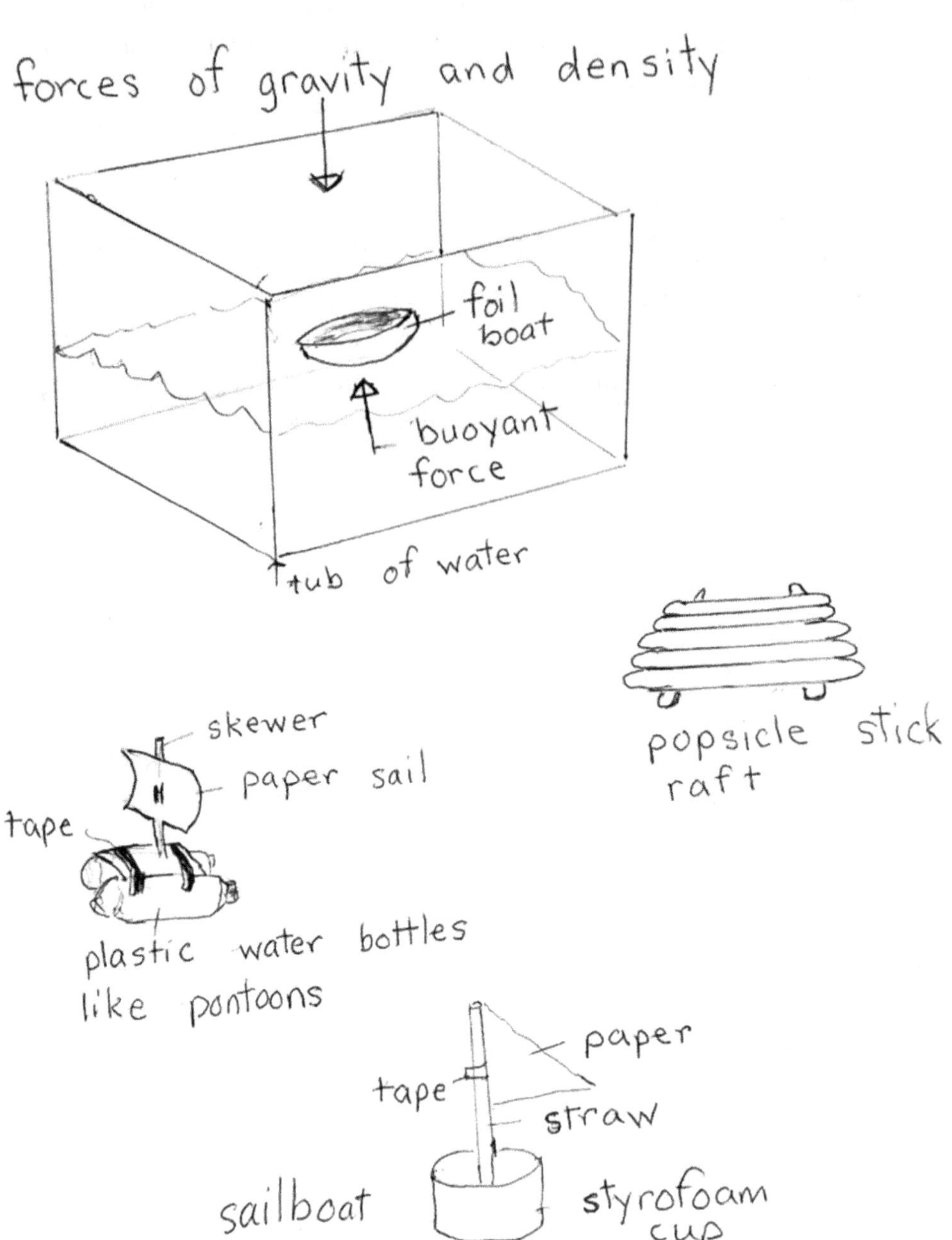

Chapter 8
Bridges

The next category of STEM challenges is bridges. Again, there are many variations and a bridge study can last at least a month of Fridays. Every time the students build with a different material they will find that due to the properties of that material, there are different types of problems to overcome. The truss bridge can be built with drinking straws, cotton swabs, or craft sticks that are connected with tape. Some materials are more flexible than others, some have more tensile strength, some are longer or thicker, and building with each type is different each time. Sometimes the bridge will be tested by placing weight on top of it that pushes down from gravitational force and other times the strength is tested by hanging a cup of weights from a string clipped to the middle and is pulled down.

You can either read the following background information or have students research the topic. Bridges come in different shapes and sizes. They have been around for thousands of years and have given people the ability to cross rivers, streams, canyons, and even to small islands off the coasts of countries. They are made up of different materials such as stone, steel, wood, and concrete and any combinations of those.

Architects design bridges by drawing out their design on paper or a computer, they then make a small-scale model of the bridge they are creating, and finally they actually build the bridge itself. They usually have a design team of engineers they collaborate with about ideas. When bridges are constructed, they have to be tested to see whether they are safe and strong enough to hold a lot of weight and can withstand the elements of nature like wind, rain, snow, earthquakes, etc.

Bridges are an important engineering design that people use every day around the world. They can be as simple as a large tree placed across a small river to as complicated as a gigantic structure with thousands of cables, beams, and wires allowing many cars and trucks to cross at once. Engineers must carefully design a bridge so that it will not collapse because of too much weight, not enough support, strong winds or flooding.

There are different types of bridges. A beam bridge is the simplest and spans two flat surfaces with a flat surface, like a board across the ditch to get to the mailbox. An arch bridge has a curve under the flat surface to provide more support underneath and is often seen supporting an elevated train track. A tied arch bridge has the arch on top and columns underneath. A truss bridge has a series of triangles incorporated into its structure. A suspension bridge has two towers tied together with parallel wires and then vertical wires attached from that horizontal, which actually will start to sag, to the flat surface that is hanging or suspended between the towers. A famous example is the Golden Gate Bridge in California.

A cable-stayed bridge also has a tower or pole and wires that come straight to the bridge surface and create larger and larger triangles. The cantilever bridge is like a drawbridge and can be lifted from the base and opened like a door or a double door to allow taller ships to cross without crashing into the bridge.

The construction of the towers should come to mind because a bridge is a similar structure just with a different orientation. Instead of going up, a bridge must go out. It must span from one side of the river or abyss to the other side. The materials you tried for the towers can now be adapted for the bridges. The bridge my students made with ear swabs and tape for Halloween was called a "bone bridge" because of the white color and the way they bulb on each end to remind one of bones in skeletons. We did not really build a bridge of bones, yuck. Change up the materials and you can build bridges for a month of Fridays. You can try straws, or skewers, or craft sticks, or K-nex, and lots of masking tape.

Example: **STEM Challenge—Engineering a Paper Beam Bridge**

I can build a paper bridge that will hold the most weight.

ETS1-1. Define a simple design problem reflecting a need or a want that includes specified criteria for success and constraints on materials, time, or cost.

ETS1-2. Generate and compare multiple possible solutions to a problem based on how well each is likely to meet the criteria and constraints of the problem.

ETS1-3. Plan and carry out fair tests in which variables are controlled and failure points are considered to identify aspects of a model or prototype that can be improved.

Materials: Each group gets 2 pieces copier paper, 2 pieces of construction paper, masking tape, and 10 pennies. The material needed to test it is two stacks of books that are at least 5 cm high and seven inches apart and the bridge may not be taped down to the books.

Safety: Place pennies on the bridge one at a time until it collapses or you run out of pennies.
Work with your team in a positive manner with cooperation and kindness.

Problem: Design and build a prototype of a beam bridge that will span seven inches and support at least 10 pennies.

Imagine solutions by thinking of bridges you have seen or built

Design: each team member draws a plan on white paper for a paper bridge.

Share **plans** and note the good ideas of each to combine into a team endeavor.

Create: Build Bridges: Begin by placing a piece of paper without folding it in any way so that it sits on top of the two stacks of books at least 5 cm off the table. Make sure the books are seven inches apart. That is the simplest beam bridge. How many pennies will it hold before it sags or falls and touches the table, or pennies slide off? Try adding more paper, folding the paper, and placing tape on the bridge itself, but not the books or table, until you have a bridge that will support 10 pennies.

Test: When construction time is over. Have teams bring their bridge to the testing area that has 2 stacks of books 5cm tall and seven inches apart. One at a time have teams span the books and add pennies. Every bridge that holds 10 pennies is a success, but then pose the challenge to see which one would hold the most pennies. The distance between the books is based on the length of a common piece of copy paper which 8 ½ inches. If you have longer paper the span should also be longer.

Analyze: Compare each bridge and discuss strengths and weaknesses.

Variations

STEM Challenge—Truss Bridge

ETS1-1. Define a simple design problem reflecting a need or a want that includes specified criteria for success and constraints on materials, time, or cost.

ETS1-2. Generate and compare multiple possible solutions to a problem based on how well each is likely to meet the criteria and constraints of the problem.

ETS1-3. Plan and carry out fair tests in which variables are controlled and failure points are considered to identify aspects of a model or prototype that can be improved.

Materials: Straws, scissors, tape and to test you will need two desks 30 cm apart and a cup to hold a weight in the middle either placed on top or hanging from a string clipped on under the bridge, then add pennies until the bridge fails.

Problem: There is a gap between two surfaces that must be connected with a bridge. Your team is to design a prototype of a truss bridge that will span 30 cm. and hold a suspended weight.

Imagine what truss bridges you have seen or built with triangles to support it. Research real bridges if you lack any experience.

Plan/Design by drawing a truss bridge on paper and then getting with other team members to keep the good ideas and combine them into a team model.

Create by building the bridge with straws and tape with enough sections to span 30 cm

Test by bringing each team's bridge to see if it spans 30 centimeters and that means success of the criteria. Then hang the cup with a string and paperclip from the bottom of the bridge and begin to add pennies until it sags to the point of sliding off the desks or breaks or you run out of pennies.

Analyze the differences in the bridges such as the number of straws, where the tape was used, how big the triangles were, how long the straws were in each section, etc. How the bridge was constructed that held the most weight?

Redesign, and Retest with the same materials as time allows or move on to other materials.

Variations on this variation: for construction on following Fridays. Other types of materials for bridge construction would be similar to the towers. One material for the long sections of the shapes like a triangle and one material to connect those sections like tape. Always follow the engineering design process.

Problem-> Imagine-> Design-> Create-> Test-> Analyze

Bridge variation I like to call the **Bone Bridge Challenge**

Materials: 30 Ear swabs (like Q-tips), scissors, tape and to test you will need two surfaces 30 cm apart and high enough to hang a cup below to hold a weight in the middle either placed on top or hanging from a string clipped on under the bridge, then add pennies until the bridge fails.

Follow the previous steps of the truss bridge

STEM Challenge—Suspension Bridge (Like Golden Gate)

I can build a bridge out of recyclable materials that will be able to hold the most weight.

ETS1-1. Define a simple design problem reflecting a need or a want that includes specified criteria for success and constraints on materials, time, or cost.

ETS1-2. Generate and compare multiple possible solutions to a problem based on how well each is likely to meet the criteria and constraints of the problem.

ETS1-3. Plan and carry out fair tests in which variables are controlled and failure points are considered to identify aspects of a model or prototype that can be improved.

Materials: cereal or some other small cardboard box, 4 empty toilet paper or paper towel tubes, tape, yarn or twine, small rubber bands, hole punch, scissors, and construction paper.

Background Knowledge or Big Ideas: A suspension bridge is a bridge in which the deck (the part that you drive across) is hung from vertical cables tied onto horizontal cables suspended from towers or walls or poles. The suspension style design allows for longer spans, reduced construction costs because of reduced materials, and improved flexibility and structural integrity during earthquakes. Each cable is made up of thousands of individual steel wires that are bound together. Steel's tensile strength improves as it is stretched into wires, so these flexible cables are stronger than a solid piece of steel of the same size.

Science/Math Concepts: Most suspension bridges are built with two to four tall towers and a cable that travels from one shore, through the tower(s) on one side, and to the other tower(s) on the opposite shore. Vertical suspender cables are connected and hang from the main horizontal cable to hold the weight of the bridge deck (the flat part). The weight of the deck is supported by carefully balanced forces on the two towers. The force pulling inward on the towers is equal to the force pulling outward on the towers toward land. Because the forces are balanced, the weight pulls straight down into the towers and into the ground.

Safety: Walk with scissors down and cut away from your body.

Work with your team in a positive manner with cooperation and kindness.

Gather material and explain the **problem** of crossing a river or valley needing a bridge.

Imagine solutions by reading the background information about a suspension type of bridge.

Design: each team member draws a plan on white paper for a suspension bridge.

Share **plans** and note the good ideas of each to combine into a team endeavor.

Create bridges: If this is a competition then the materials will be a constraint and the same for every team, then the bridge that holds the most weight wins.

If this is not a competition then the materials will be only limited by what is available and if the bridge supports a small model car then it is a winner.

Another constraint is time. Planning takes time, construction takes time, and testing takes time, but it is always best if there is time for a redesign and retest for the bridge to be analyzed by the team members.

Test: Place small model cars on each bridge

Analyze the differences in the bridges such as the number of towers, where the tape was used, how long the suspension cables were, how long the vertical lines were in each section, etc. How the bridge was constructed that held the most weight?

This would be a great challenge to revisit the 4C's because there is a lot of room for creativity when recycled and found materials are used. There is a need for more collaboration and critical thinking when the task is more complicated. Ask for examples of good communication in your discourse following the challenges.

Tacoma Narrows Bridge is a suspension bridge nicknamed Galloping Gertie that collapsed due to aero elastic flutter. The bridge design failed to allow wind to pass through and the deck began oscillating in high winds, ultimately causing its collapse. Check out its video.

Bridges

Beam Bridge

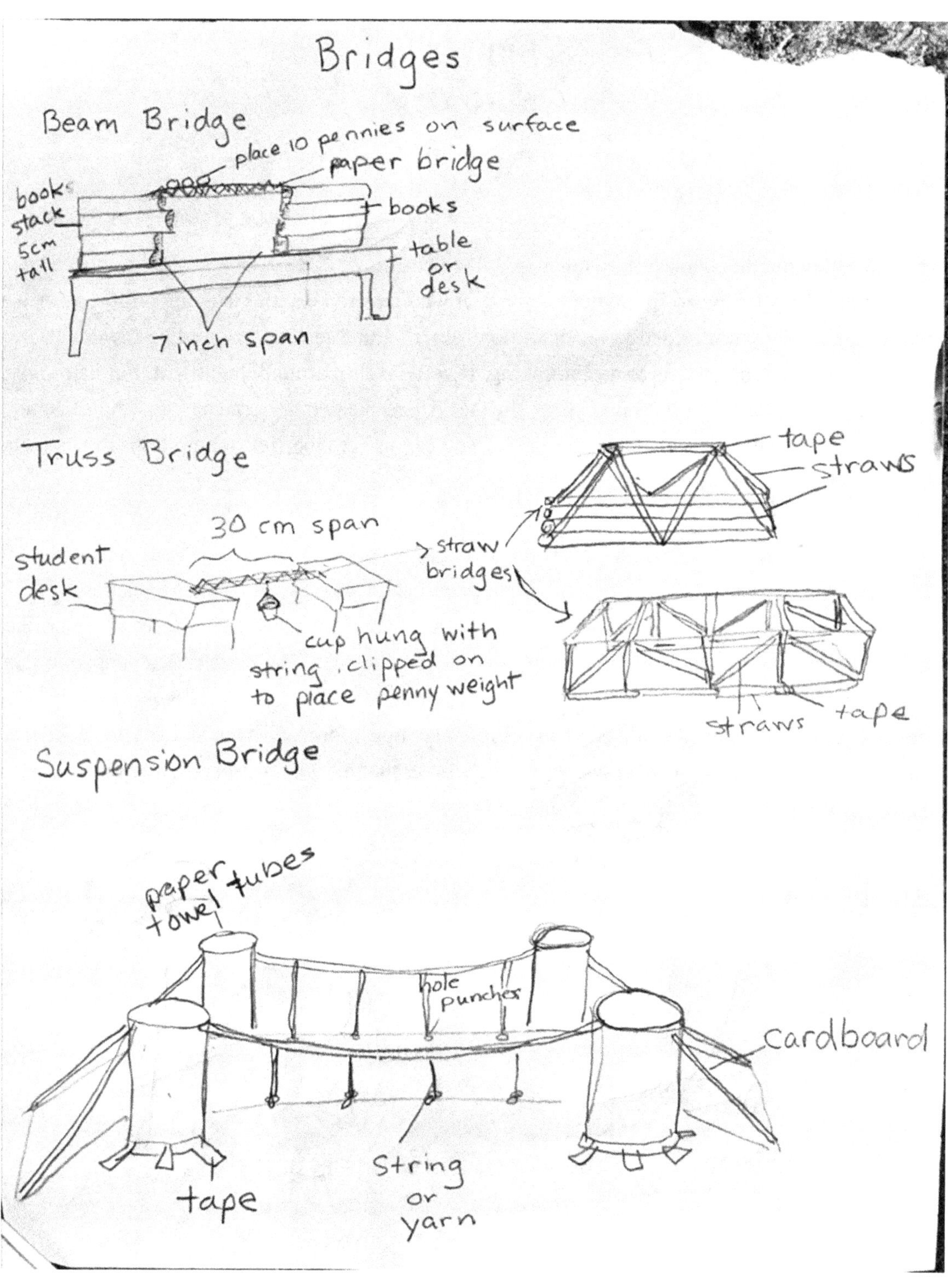

Chapter 9
Catapults

If you have been following this book of ideas then you have built towers, cars, boats, and bridges. Structures are built and tested and then you have to figure out a system of who gets to keep the winning prototype or what to do with the wreckage. Maybe you decided in the first month to alternate instead of building towers all month you went to cars. It is the iteration that gets to deep thinking. If you did skip around that is fine, but I strongly suggest revisiting tower-building for more than one week. In fact, since elementary teachers use the seasons to teach different units I think a tower for each season is perfect. You can use cranberries or gumdrops in December as the vertex between toothpicks and jellybeans around Easter.

One thing I did not mention was one fun way to destroy the towers once built is designing a wrecking ball. You can put a tennis ball in the toe of a tube sock and swing away or build a device if your students are up to the challenge. I prefer catapults. The towers of castles were demolished with catapults and trebuchets years ago. The real-world problem addressed by catapults was how to break or breach the enemy's fortress. There have been ancient catapults found that could hurl a 350 pound stone over 300 feet. The Greeks, Romans, and Chinese all used catapults in warfare.

The science and math behind catapults is about simple machines, force, energy, and angles. A fulcrum is any pivotal point that supports a lever. A lever is a long sturdy body that rests on a support (fulcrum). The load is the object being lifted or affected. See the illustration.

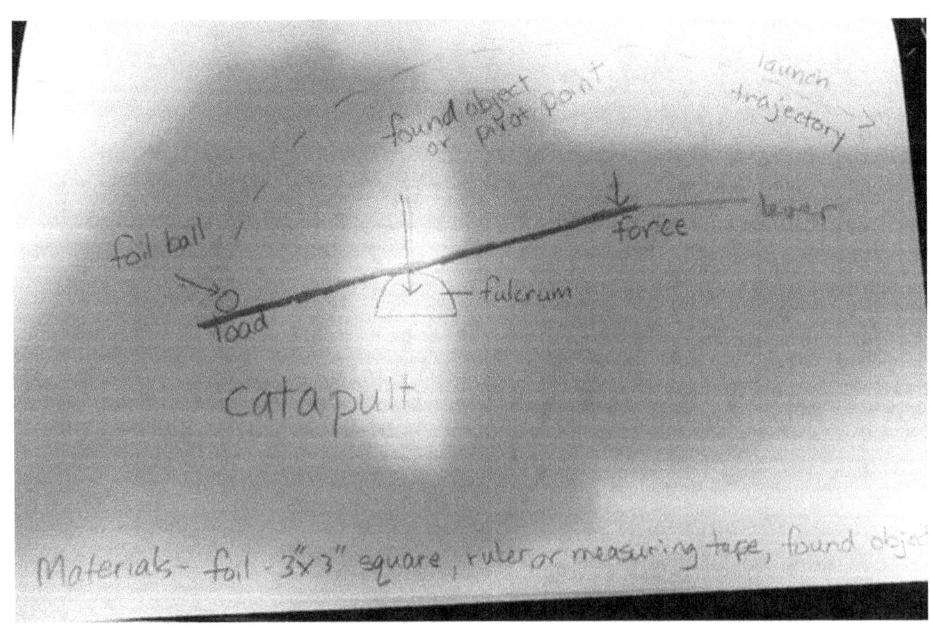

The load has potential energy stored in it and increased when force is applied in the downward push. When released it changes into kinetic energy and launches the load. Then gravity pulls downward on the load until it returns to the ground creating an arc. The trajectory depends on the weight of the load and the force on the lever over the fulcrum.

Example: **STEM Challenge—Catapults**

I can build a catapult from found materials that will launch a foil ball the farthest.

3-5-ETS1-1. Define a simple design problem reflecting a need or a want that includes specified criteria for success and constraints on materials, time, or cost.

3-5-ETS1-2. Generate and compare multiple possible solutions to a problem based on how well each is likely to meet the criteria and constraints of the problem.

3-5-ETS1-3. Plan and carry out fair tests in which variables are controlled and failure points are considered to identify aspects of a model or prototype that can be improved.

Materials: Each group gets: 3" x 3" pieces of aluminum foil to smash into a ball, masking tape, some found materials to create a fulcrum, a lever, and a bucket or sling on one end of the arm of the lever. Group testing material: an open area to launch and a meter stick or measuring tape to measure the distance.

Safety: Launch and measure only when everyone on the team is ready

Problem: We need a prototype of a catapult

Imagine solutions by thinking of catapults you have seen or built

Design: each team member draws a plan on white paper for a catapult including the material your team found

Share plans and note the good ideas of each to combine into a team endeavor.

Create catapults: The lever can be anything long and sturdy that is also flat enough (ruler, paint stick, spoon, pencil, etc.) to balance the foil ball until launch time. A small container (water bottle or Gatorade lid, medicine cap, etc.) can be taped onto one end of the lever to hold the load in place. The fulcrum can be anything small that the lever can rest on top of once placed under the middle such as a block or a hemisphere shaped object (playdough or a wad of paper). The parts of the catapult are only limited by the available material and team imagination.

Test: The catapults can be tested all at once, but are more easily measured one at a time. Place the catapult at a designated spot. Place the foil ball on the lever. Countdown 3, 2, 1, Launch by pushing down the elevated arm of the lever and release quickly. Measure the distance it landed from the catapult.

Analyze: Compare each catapult and discuss strengths and weaknesses. Redesign and retest as often as time allows.

Variations

Catapult Variation 1—**Target Catapult**

Change the materials and this becomes a new STEM lesson because of the properties of the new material. One way to change this basic idea is to draw a target with sidewalk chalk on the floor or on the playground blacktop outside and have teams try to launch pompons or foil balls for the most points, sort of like lawn darts. The bullseye target would have concentric circles labeled with points. This time the problem would be precision more than distance. The points should increase as the circumference of the circles decreases, so that the smallest circle is worth the most points. The weight and size of the load may be a variable to consider as precision is more important, so they can use more or less foil. There may be a starting line that teams are not allowed to cross, but may place their catapult as far away as space allows to explore the force and trajectory needed to land within the target at desired points.

One constraint could be that each team will get three launches and either gets the largest points earned or the sum of all three. Decide beforehand or have one game for each. If the large target and larger distance is a problem with available found materials just adjust the size of the target like drawing it on a piece of paper to place inches away instead of feet.

This is a new problem so let us see how it fits the engineering design process

Problem-> Imagine-> Design-> Create-> Test-> Analyze

Problem: There is a toy company that wants to have new toy catapult to market.

Imagine what types of toys you have seen that use a type of catapult like the one that throws pie in your face

Design by drawing your ideas on paper using the found materials your team acquired

Create by building the catapults

Test by bringing each team's catapult to the starting line. Remember the team does not have to set up exactly on the line, but may not cross it. Launch the ball or pompon (bean bags would not roll and be easier to assess the point value if they are available, but that means the catapults must be larger). Each team gets their turn and a total of three launches.

Analyze each launch and make adjustments between. Add up the points and compare between the different styles of catapults the teams were able to create as well as the process they used.

Catapult Variation 2 **Field Goal Catapult**

During football season, construct a field goal post from straws or other found material and the launches even need to be more precise. The foil ball or pompon represents a football and the challenge would be using the catapult to launch it between the posts from the farthest distance. Older students may know how to fold a classic paper folded football and that can be their load. You may even create a football field with lines parallel to the goal line representing the yard lines on the gridiron. The scoring variation can be 3 points for each launch that passes through the uprights after 3 launches. Or the points from the yard lines that increase the farther you get from the goal line up to 50.

Problem-> Imagine-> Design-> Create-> Test-> Analyze

Problem: There is another toy company that has approached you to make a new toy with the same catapult principle to appeal to the football fans as potential customers.

Imagine what a kicker does with his leg as a lever and the holder as the fulcrum and other toys like those that hit ping-pong balls to shoot through hoops

Design by drawing your plans on paper and collaborating with team members to decide together what your toy will look like

Create by building the football catapult

Test by bringing each team's catapult to the field goal yard line. Every team that gets their football to go through the straw uprights gets to try again but from a farther distance until there is a catapult that is able to kick the football through from the farthest distance consistently.

Analyze each catapult prototype and make adjustments as you go along. In the discourse that follows compare and contrast each team's catapult and the process they used to prepare for the kick off.

Catapult Variation 3 **Basketball Catapult**

During basketball season, use an empty bowl or basket on the floor or a desk that is the goal for the ball to land in for scoring points. Teams may use the same catapults repeatedly with slight adjustments or completely build new catapults each time. Teams may use foil balls, pompons, small bouncy balls, Ping-Pong balls, etc. Scoring can be 1 point from a designated free throw line or 2 points from certain distances and 3 points from farther away from the basket and the constraint is that they get only 5 shots. Or if it is the time of indoor recesses because of cold weather or March Madness you could play H-O-R-S-E until only one team remains. The rules of Horse are that the first team that makes a basket sets the criteria that following teams must also get their ball in the basket or earn a letter. If a team spells out horse they are eliminated. The winner is the last team left that has not completely spelled out horse.

Problem-> Imagine-> Design-> Create-> Test-> Analyze

Problem: The toy company now wants to get a toy catapult marketed that will appeal to the basketball fans out there

Imagine what worked with catapults to improve precision

Design by drawing a prototype model of a basketball catapult and discuss with your team how it works to compromise for a team design

Create by building the basketball catapult toy

Test by bringing each team's catapult to the free throw line and every successful basket earns points 1 at the line 2 anywhere else, but you may want to draw a line that represents the 3 point shots. Every team gets five shots and the total points from those shots.

Analyze the differences in the catapults and the process each team used to create their toys

In the discourse following any of the catapult challenges, you should revisit the 4 C's. Ask for examples from students or point out the moments you observed while teams followed the design process. What is one example of creativity in this challenge? What is an example of good communication? What is an example of good collaboration? During the analyze step we hear a lot of examples of critical thinking, but what happened during the test, redesign, and retest that illustrates critical thinking.

Catapult Challenges

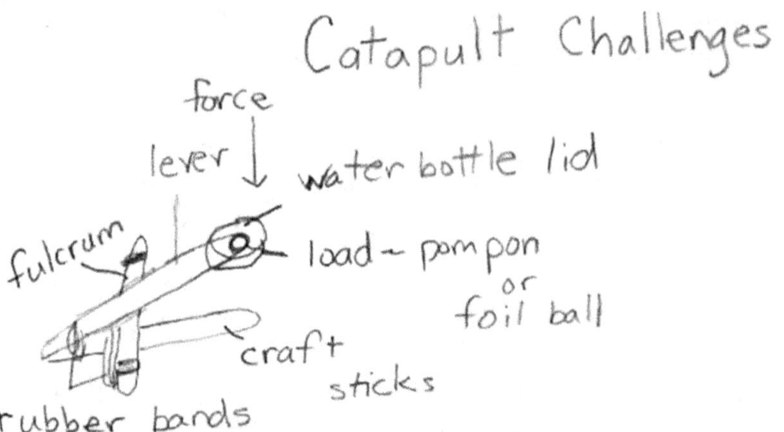

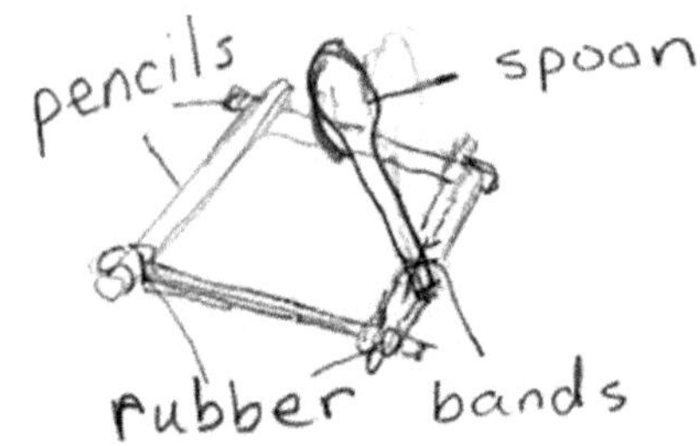

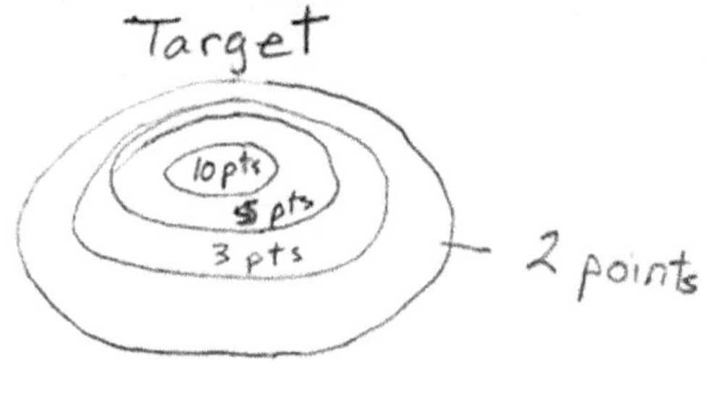

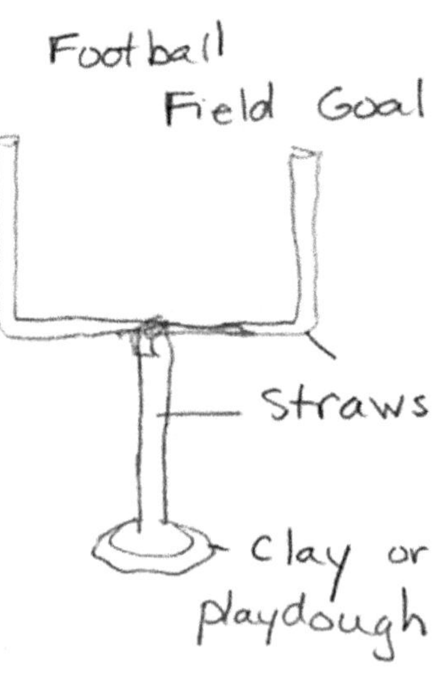

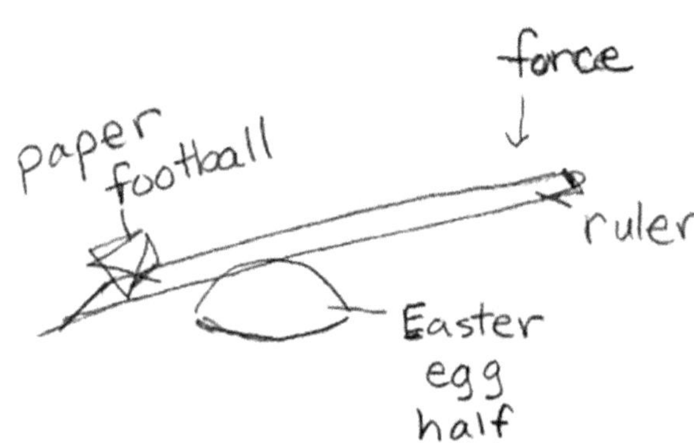

Chapter 10
Planes

This next category is planes. One book that you could read aloud to kick off the unit is the 1984 Caldecott winner *The Glorious Flight : Across the Channel with Louis Blériot* by Alice and Martin Provensen. I love all the Caldecott books with their beautiful illustrations, but I especially like the ones that tell a great story as well.

There is some background information for your STEM endeavors into flight. As always the background is meant to set the stage historically, presenting the problems that were solved through engineering. It is also to attempt a basic explanation of some of the math and science concepts involved that may help students and teachers understand the phenomena they will experience while having fun learning.

Aviation in general has helped tourism, trade, connectivity, and economic growth. Those in the aviation industry also believes it provides jobs, improves living standards, alleviates poverty, provides a lifeline for remote communities, enables a rapid response when disasters occur, and helps drive the development of the modern world. All of these are real-world problems that have been solved with the invention of planes and helicopters.

So look at flight another way and show how the ability to fly has solved real-life problems. The Kansas City Chiefs play teams all over the country. They would have to ride a bus and drive for hours, even days to get to the city of their opponents and that would keep them from staying in shape and practicing plays. When they fly, they get there in a matter of hours.

Hawaii has eight major islands and hundreds of others, so to travel between them boats take hours, but planes can cut that time so if there was a need to evacuate for volcanic eruptions then a plane would be the way to go.

Hikers and soldiers get themselves into remote locations all the time. Whenever there is a life-threatening situation for one of them a helicopter can buzz in and transport them to the helipad of the nearest hospital.

Since the beginning of time, man could crawl, walk, swim, run, jump, and the only mobility of other life forms he did not have was the ability to fly. That itself can even be the problem, the desire to see the earth from above. The bird's eye view can solve a whole list of other problems, such as, mapping and planning pathways. Man's desire to fly may have started with jealousy, but once it was accomplished it was put to good use.

Lighter than air things like balloons float rather than fly. Hot air balloons float on air like life rafts float on water because of buoyancy and density principles (that were covered in the Boat chapter, so you may need to look at that again). The raft is less dense than the water so it floats. Heating the air in a balloon makes the air inside it less dense than the air in the atmosphere, so it rises and floats.

Kites and gliders use the ideas of wind resistance and air pressure to appear to fly up off the ground. Models of them have appeared in records from history, think about Leonardo Da Vinci and Ben Franklin. There are many important dates in aviation history, but I will just mention a few more. You are welcome to research and expand this unit as you see fit and I have not even touched on rocketry and flying into space, which could be another category. In 1852 a steam powered air ship called a dirigible was controlled and flown for seventeen miles. In 1903 the Wright brothers flew their gas powered biplane in Kitty Hawk, North Carolina. The first helicopter was flown in 1907.

The theory of flight for things that are not lighter than air involve the principles of lift, gravity, drag, and thrust. It is the balance of all these forces that enables something to fly. The upward force of lift must be greater than the downward force of gravity. The forward force of thrust must be greater than the backward force of drag. See how NASA illustrates it.

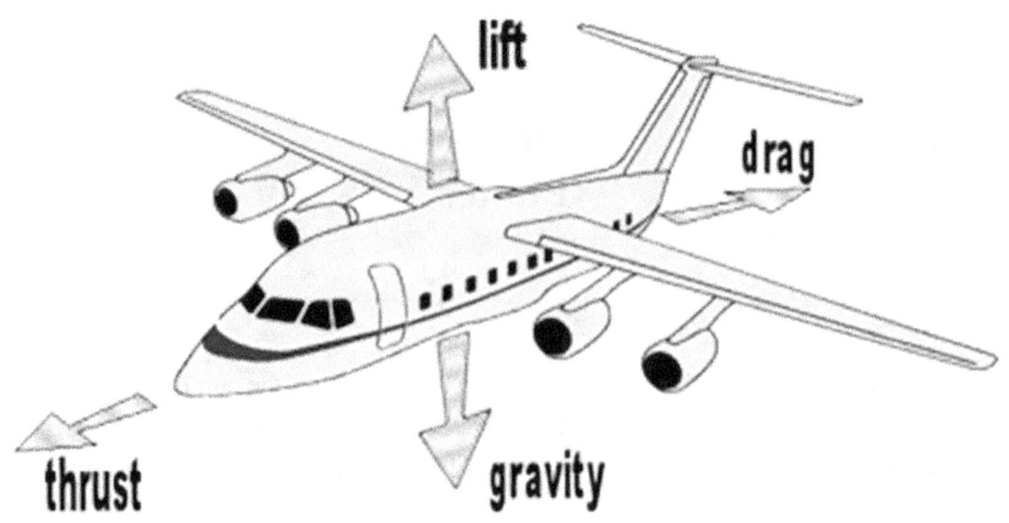

https://www.grc.nasa.gov/www/k-12/UEET/StudentSite/dynamicsofflight.html

Many of your students will have experience folding paper into a paper airplane, but not all. I would have students raise their hand if they have experience and those who have not partner up with someone who has, until everyone has a partner or at least someone in their group that has experience. The younger students may need you to actually fold a prototype together. The experience they will lack will be using different types of paper. Engineering is often a test of materials needed for certain structures or products.

The paper airplane STEM challenge is okay for partners or teams of three, but any more and it is difficult to keep all engaged. After exploring with copier paper to try out different ways to fold paper airplanes you should prohibit that type of paper for the challenge. Any type of other paper should be made available, such as, **wrapping paper, notebook paper, construction paper, wax paper, aluminum foil, parchment paper, etc. Other plane construction material to offer: masking tape, paper clips, staples, scotch tape, duct tape.**

Read the challenge problem and exhibit all the construction material available.

Paper Airplanes for Penny Passengers

Problem: There is no copier paper available to make paper airplanes, so which type of paper will carry the most penny passengers the farthest?

Imagine: What type of gliders and paper airplanes can overcome the lift and drag forces to fly the farthest and how can you attach penny passengers?

Design: Draw the types of paper airplanes your team would like to try with an example of how to attach passengers, and discuss as a team which two you will try first.

Create: You have 5 minutes to create your first two planes.

Test: Fly the planes in the designated area without any pennies attached with different types of launching. One partner is at the starting line and one is downfield to retrieve the plane once it lands to fly it back to the starter.

Analyze: Measure the longest flight and add a penny to retest. You have 10 minutes to select one plane to compete against all the other teams.

Class competition begins by adding one penny to each plane for flight testing. The plane that flies the farthest gets a point. Add another penny to each plane, fly in the designated area either all at once if space allows, or one at a time if needed. The plane that flies the farthest gets a point.

Add another penny to each plane, fly, measure and farthest flown gets the point. At least three penny passengers must successfully stay on the plane throughout the entire flight. There can be analyzing time after each flight as a class, but at the very least by each team. There can be adjustments made between each flight like a pit stop during a car race, but if the plane is not at the starting line at test time they will lose the opportunity to earn a point for that round, but may join in the next round of testing.

The next iteration is also a glider. Flying machine number two is called a Straw Glider. The same forces apply, lift versus gravity and thrust versus drag. The teams can be 2-3 students and now they all have experience with gliders, so a random team selection would work.

The only material to add is a drinking straw which must be the plane's body or fuselage. The fuselage of an aircraft is the long hollow body that holds all the other parts of the plane together. The fuselage is the part that holds the cargo or passengers and to which the tail and wings are connected.

Plane Variation 1—**Straw Glider**

Straw Glider

Materials for each team are: tape, scissors, one piece of copier paper, one drinking straw.

Problem: Create a glider with a drinking straw as the body that will fly the farthest?
Imagine: What type of gliders and paper airplanes overcome the lift and drag forces to fly the farthest? What is attached to the fuselage of airplanes? Wings? Tails?
Design: Plan with drawings of possible ways to use the available materials to construct a glider.
Create: You have 5 minutes to create your team glider.
Test: Fly the gliders in the designated area. One partner is at the starting line and one is downfield to retrieve the glider once it lands to fly it back to the starter.
Analyze: Analyze the flight and redesign the parts and test, repeat until you have achieved the longest flight or run out of time.

The class should get together to see each team's glider and demonstrate how each flies. The time should be spent for each team to analyze their own gliders and share their process when the class gets together. This would be a great time to review the 4 C's and ask for examples the students felt exhibited each skill throughout their process. Ask for examples of creativity, collaboration, communication and critical thinking.

The next iteration of the plane category piggybacks off the other two. It is called Ring Flyer. You may google it to see examples, but I would not show it to students until after the first tests and analyzing steps. Each team will have the same materials available. The straw should have two rings attached instead of wings. The rings are loops of paper. The loops can be the same circumference or different. The loops can be the same width or different. The loops can be the same type of paper or different. The google examples have one large loop attached to one end of the straw and one smaller loop attached to the other end. That may limit the creativity if you show it beforehand.

Plane Variation 2—**Ring Flyers**

Ring Flyers

Materials for each team are: tape, scissors, one drinking straw, different types of paper such as, wrapping paper, notebook paper, construction paper, wax paper, aluminum foil, parchment paper, etc.

Problem: Create a glider with a drinking straw as the body and only rings as wings that will fly the farthest?
Imagine: What type of gliders and paper airplanes overcome the lift and drag forces to fly the farthest? What is attached to the fuselage of airplanes?

Design: Plan with drawings of possible ways to use the available materials to construct a ring glider.

Create: You have 5 minutes to create your team ring glider.

Test: Fly the gliders in the designated area. One partner is at the starting line and one is downfield to retrieve the glider once it lands to fly it back to the starter.

Analyze: Analyze the flight and redesign the parts and test, repeat until you have achieved the longest flight or run out of time.

The class should get together to see each team's ring straw glider and demonstrate how each flies. The time should be spent for each team to analyze their own gliders and share their process when the class gets together. Review the 4 C's and ask for examples the students felt exhibited each skill throughout their process. Ask for examples of creativity, collaboration, communication and critical thinking.

The final iteration for the plane category is a launcher prototype. The launcher is really a type of catapult, so the students have some experience. They will be constructing paper airplanes and adding a hook to the nose which in turn gets hooked onto a rubber band, so the plane will need to have a sturdy nose. Teams should construct more than one plane in case the nose crumples and bends. They will hook the paper clip on the nose of a plane around a rubber band, and pull it back to stretch the rubber band. Aim the plane forward and release. Their job is to create the device that holds the rubber band we will call the launcher.

In real life, the launchers are on aircraft carriers. The problem of getting planes across oceans with enough gas to fly where the battles are on land is solved when the planes ride on a boat first, and then take off and land on that boat. The boats are called aircraft carriers. In order to take off, an airplane has to generate enough lift or upward force due to air pushing on the plane to overcome its weight. Weight is really another word for gravity since the downward force is due to gravity. The faster an airplane goes, the more lift it generates. This is why airport runways are usually very long when they are on land. They can be longer than a mile because planes need a lot of space to gain enough speed or thrust to take off. They also need a lot of space to land safely and stop from such high speeds.

Aircraft carriers are large ships with runways on them that allow aircraft to take off and land in the open ocean. Although aircraft carriers are huge compared with most other ships, they are still small compared to land-based airports and runways. Airplanes can't gain enough speed to take off on their own over such a short distance, so they get an extra boost from a type of catapult on the deck of the ship. This catapult provides extra energy from a source such as compressed air or electromagnets to help the plane gain extra speed. The catapult hooks on to the plane and helps it accelerate over the shorter distance so that it can get enough speed (thrust) and lift to take off. Another science concept to mention about this STEM challenge is that the rubber band stores potential energy, which gives extra kinetic energy or moving energy to the airplane.

Instead of building an aircraft carrier the paper airplane launcher will resemble more of a slingshot. Students that have seen the movies about *Top Gun* have an idea in mind what an aircraft carrier looks like.

Variation 3—**Airplane Launcher**

Airplane Launcher

Materials: different types of paper to build the airplanes, paper clips, rubber bands, tape, and recycled materials like cardboard and plastic to build the launchers. You can also let them use Legos or other building materials if they are available.

Use the engineering design process to build a more permanent launcher for your team's airplane.

Problem: Create a paper airplane with a launcher that will fly the farthest?

Imagine: What type of paper will be strong enough not to crumple or rip when pulled back on the rubber band? What type of launcher will work best, stationary or handheld?

Design: Plan with drawings of possible ways to use the available materials to construct a launcher device that will support the rubber band.

Create: You have ten minutes to create your team planes and launcher.

Test: Launch the planes in the designated area. Place the launcher at the starting line. Place the paper clip hook on the nose of the plane onto the rubber band and pull back toward your launching teammate and release. Measure the distance.

Analyze: Analyze the flight. Can you pull back farther or make the launcher steadier and clear of obstacles? Is the hook working? Redesign any parts and retest, repeat until you have achieved the longest flight or run out of time.

Get the teams together to analyze together. Their process. Compare and contrast the team's planes and launchers. Review the 4 C's and ask for examples the students felt exhibited each skill throughout their process. Ask for examples of creativity, collaboration, communication and critical thinking.

The flight theme could last another month of Fridays with kites, parachutes, rockets, hovercrafts, and helicopters. There may be even enough of those challenges to write another book. Let me know if that interests you and I will start that journey. Flight has always fascinated me and I have sponsored many a Young Astronauts Club.

+++++++++++++++

Planes & Gliders

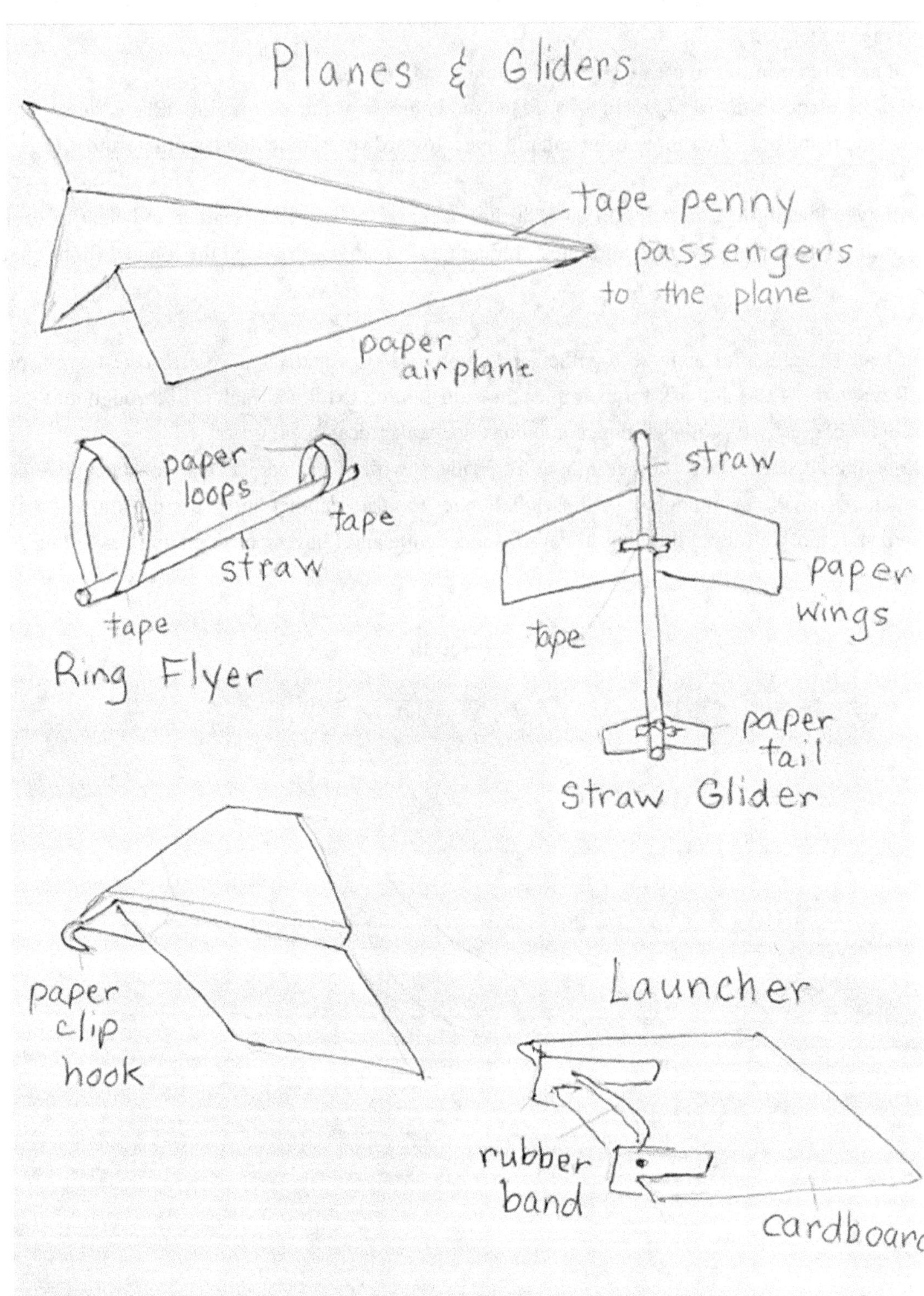

Chapter 11
Marble Mazes

A maze is a network of paths. Mazes are usually designed as a puzzle through which something has to find their way. Most mazes also have a start and a finish. The hedge mazes in Europe were popular in gardens. One famous maze is the Dole Pineapple Maze that is located in Hawaii. People walk through this huge maze trying to find their way into the center to find the giant pineapple. Mazes are also made in cornfields in the fall students may have experienced.

The difference between a maze from a labyrinth is that a labyrinth has a unicursal path that if followed will lead you to the center. A maze however can have several dead ends. The maze hedges and corn are grown tall enough so that visitors cannot see anything but the path in front of them winding around in confusing circles branching out in different directions. The purpose is mostly for challenging fun, but adds a sense of secrecy and mystery. Sometimes it is even a race.

This challenge may require some research in the planning step of the engineering process. You may wish to review the laws of motion with students before they draw their designs. Just simply put, things in motion stay in motion unless an outside force acts upon it. One of the outside forces is always gravity. Gravity is invisible and constant, so you have to remind students by asking them why we are not floating around in space. Remind them that gravity pulls things down toward the center of earth. Gravity pulls on everything, the desk, the chair, and the marble also. Marble tracks or marble runs work on the principle that once a marble is dropped at the top it will move downward because of gravity. The toymakers that fashioned tubes and curves and spins slowed that path downward with interesting motion. If any are available, they are fun to explore motion, but are really not a STEM challenge unless you introduce constraints and work in teams.

A review of surface area may need to be reviewed as ways to increase time or slow down a marble's descent. In other words, using all the space available takes longer to cover the ground between point A(the start) and point B(the finish), in the maze. Actually walking through a room of desks randomly spread out illustrates this point. A teacher must always keep in mind the walking paths when designing the seating arrangements in a classroom. The more surface area the better when fitting in 20-30 desks.

The downward descent may also be slowed down by putting up walls. However if the wall is not at the correct angle, it will completely stop the marble and that is not a favorable outcome. Students need to think about angles of their ramps and base. Remind them that the steeper the hills when riding a bike means the faster the bike goes when riding down and slower going up. The base or floor of the maze they are constructing will need to be raised to create that downward slope and the steeper the slant the faster the marble will roll. That can mean raising a maze that is not stationary on one end at a time, but carefully not sporadically or jerky.

The simplest mazes are built within the rims of a paper plate with straws glued down in horizontal segments for walls or loops of paper glued down like croquet brackets for tunnels. Students move the plate around to get a marble to roll the entire path. The mazes get more complex as they are built inside a box lid with straws and/or paper brackets to roll around and through, and are still manipulated by the student by tilting and raising the floor of the maze to keep the marble rolling.

The most complex maze is a stationary one created with cardboard and tape to allow a marble to freefall at the slowest pace as it rolls down one ramp, changes direction, and rolls down another ramp. Another factor to keep in mind with this challenge is friction. Friction is the force needed for one object to slide across another surface or object. The less friction means the speed is not impeded, the more friction there is the slower the motion. There are things to add to the rolling surface that can increase or decrease friction. Sandpaper or ridges are examples of surfaces that would increase friction and slow the roll. The fun climax is a maze created to represent a miniature mini-golf hole with the marble being hit with a miniature golf club. Again, the angles and friction are important to increase or decrease the par per hole.

Example: **STEM Challenge—Paper Plate Marble Maze**
I can build a maze toy from paper and cardboard for a marble to roll through

K-2 ETS 1-1 Ask questions, make observations, and gather information about a situation people want to change to define a simple problem that can be solved through the development of a new or improved object or tool.

K-2 ETS 1-2 Develop a simple sketch, drawing, or physical model to illustrate how the shape of an object helps it function as needed to solve a given problem.

K-2 ETS 1-3 Analyze data from tests of two objects designed to solve the same problem to compare the strengths and weaknesses of how each performs.

Materials: Each group gets: a paper plate, a marble, plastic straws, glue, strips of construction paper, markers, and crayons.

Safety: Keep marbles off the floor as they are a tripping hazard. Use scissors safely.
Work with your team in a positive manner with cooperation and kindness.

Problem: The toy factory is looking for a fun marble maze to sell as a challenging puzzle.
Imagine solutions by thinking of mazes you have used, seen, or built
Design: each team member draws a plan on white paper for a maze.
Share **plans** and note the good ideas of each to combine into a team endeavor.
Create mazes: The teams may be partners instead of 3-4 with easy challenges with abundant materials. Paper plates come in packs of 100 and is small enough that more than two sets of hands may not stay engaged enough. Have partners compare their ideas and combine ideas. Glue down the straws as walls to guide the marble and add a paper tunnel here and there along the maze path. Draw arrows on the plate itself for the Start and Finish areas.
Test: One fun way to test is to trade mazes with other partners and try to see if you can navigate a marble from their Start to their Finish by following the path without having the marble fall off the plate.
Analyze: Compare each maze to discuss their strengths and weaknesses. Redesign and retest.

Variations

Maze Variation 1—**30 Second Marble Maze Challenge**

3-5-ETS1-1 Define a simple design problem reflecting a need or a want that includes specified criteria for success and constraints on materials, time, or cost.

3-5-ETS1-2 Generate and compare multiple possible solutions to a problem based on how well each is likely to meet the criteria and constraints of the problem.

3-5-ETS1-3. Plan and carry out fair tests in which variables are controlled and failure points are considered to identify aspects of a model or prototype that can be improved.

Materials: Each group gets: a copier paper box lid, a marble, masking tape, boxes such as cereal that is easy to cut into strips, but strong and rigid enough to become ramps, scissors, glue, string, other found materials, stopwatch or a clock with a second hand.

Your **problem** is to design and build a marble maze that lasts at least 30 seconds from start to finish with only gravity, friction, and inertia as the acting forces. You may use the wall or stacks of books to elevate one end, but once the marble is set in motion you may not touch or support any part of the maze or marble. If the marble stops the time stops.

Imagine other mazes you have used, seen, or built. Think about skate park designs and what is used to slow down or change direction. Watch the Marble Run Challenge video

https://www.youtube.com/watch?v=IN0Wn0XgPXQ

Plan/Design the bird's eye view of a maze that uses ramps

Create Mazes by taping one side of cardboard strips to the box lid. Start at one corner of the box and tape the strip so that it is at an angle from the side designated as the top. The ramp should be built the entire width except for where the marble is intended to drop to the next ramp where it is to change direction and travel on the ramp below it at an opposing angle to the other side. Place the marble in the corner and raise that end of the lid. Watch the motion and adjust as needed to adapt the speed of the rolling marble once it is set into motion. This will take many patient hours. You may want to allow 10-minute chunks of time every day for week or two to get really complicated mazes. Each time a ramp is added the angle needs to be tested. There is a lot of critical thinking and creativity going on, so it is worth the time spent. See one example:

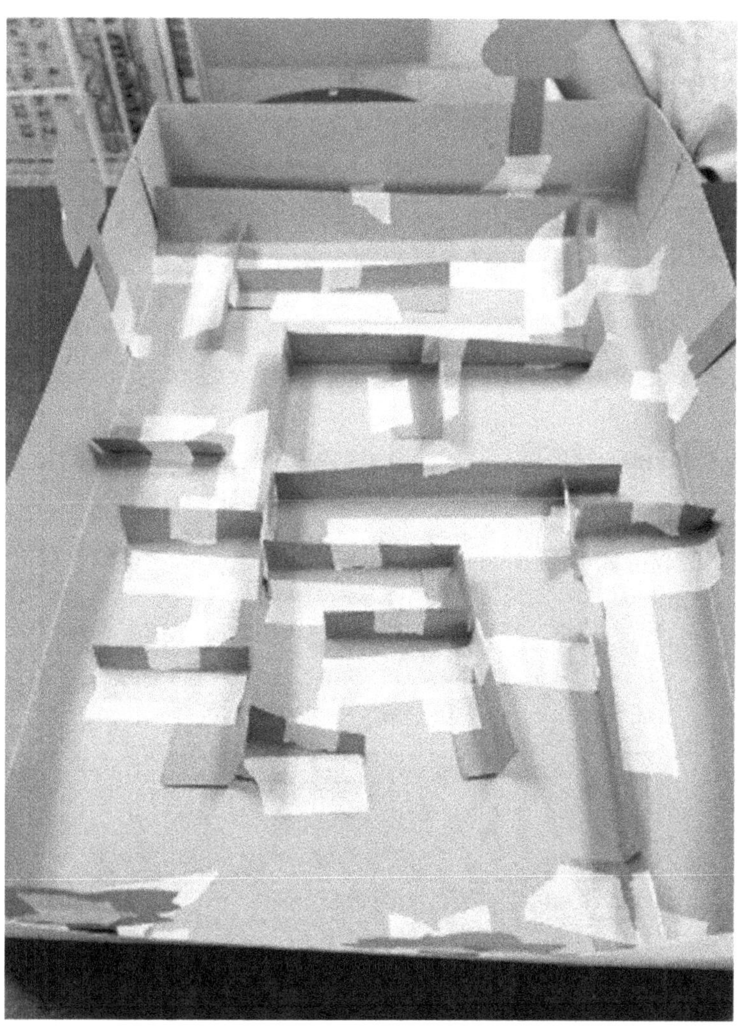

Test: Place the marble at the "Start" corner that is on the raised end (resting on a stack of books). Set the marble in motion and time how long it takes to either reach the "Finish" or stop rolling.

Analyze each marble maze to see if any were able to keep the marble moving for 30 seconds or longer. Compare the strengths and weaknesses of each maze and make adjustments to retest later.

Maze Variation 2—**Mini Miniature Golf Hole Challenge:**

3-5-ETS1-1. Define a simple design problem reflecting a need or a want that includes specified criteria for success and constraints on materials, time, or cost.

3-5-ETS1-2. Generate and compare multiple possible solutions to a problem based on how well each is likely to meet the criteria and constraints of the problem.

3-5-ETS1-3. Plan and carry out fair tests in which variables are controlled and failure points are considered to identify aspects of a model or prototype that can be improved.

Materials: Each group gets: a marble, masking tape, boxes such as shoebox that is easy to cut, scissors, glue, string, other found materials, construction paper, a craft stick or pencil to become the golf club

Problem is to design a miniature mini-golf hole with a maze and other obstacles that a marble can be pushed through using a miniature golf club.

Imagine a theme for the hole based on available material. You may need to show examples of a mini-golf course for any student that has not seen one in person.

Plan how to create a prototype for a new golf hole in which a marble is the golf ball. Think of miniature golf parks you have seen or played.

Create the golf hole that incorporates a maze and a hole. Other obstacles are encouraged, but the ball (marble) cannot be touched by anything other than the golf club (craft stick with cardboard head taped on one end). Find the average of how many hits it takes to navigate from tee (Start) to hole (Finish) to post the par suggestion.

Test: Place your marble at someone else's hole tee and see if you can get it through the mazes and other obstacles to the hole in the suggested number of hits (par). If it works then everyone feels successful.

Analyze: Was it too hard or too easy? How can it be improved? Make adaptations and line up all the holes for a classroom golf course.

Maybe there can be a theme for the entire course. Create scorecards and play a round of miniature mini-golf.

Variation 3—**Amazing Minute**

Make the 30-second maze last 60 seconds using the same design process. It may be interesting to just replicate the current 30 second model a team has and see if it adds up to 60. Or teams are welcome to start all over from scratch.

Problem—build a maze that takes a marble exactly one minute to complete

Imagine, Design, Create, Test, Analyze

Marble Mazes

Paper Plate Maze

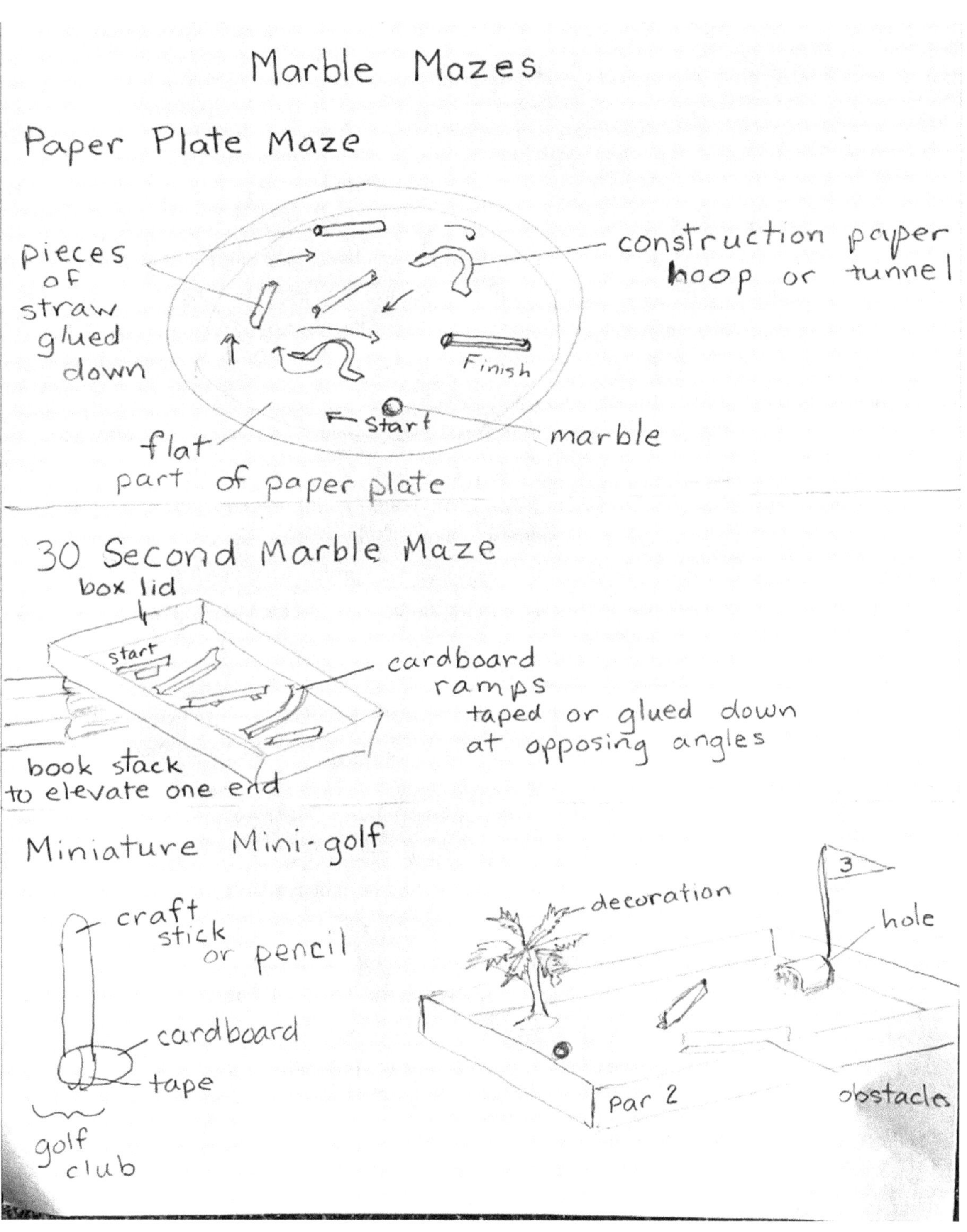

Chapter 12
Houses

This chapter category is houses. It is such a broad category that it could probably last a teacher an entire year all by itself. I will only include enough challenges for one month. Kids have been engineering "houses" since they were little when they built forts with blankets and furniture around the house. My children also used boxes and tubs to make houses for their dolls and pets for as long as I can remember. One of our favorite memories is making a fairy hut for the garden nymphs we believe live in our yard. Here is some background information to read and share or you may wish to research houses on your own.

Shelter is one of the basic human needs along with food, water, clothes, and sleep. The difference between a want and a need is a discussion for economics, but I would use the example that everyone does **need** shelter, but may **want** a mansion or beach house. There is a problem in our country with homelessness and this category may bring this issue up. What do people do today that don't have a house? They seek shelter under bridges and overpasses, caves, forests, and tents. Affordable housing is a current problem, so maybe there is a student in our classrooms today that will find a solution to this issue in the future and you are sparking that interest with these challenges.

If you teach a grade level that studies Native Americans in some manner, they are a perfect example of people using the resources that are readily available to build shelters. Tribes that lived in snow and ice made igloos. First Americans that lived in woodlands made lodges of trees. Tribes that lived on the plains made homes of animal skin, sod, buffalo dung, and rocks because that is what is found there. Those that lived in the desert made adobe bricks to build their villages. People all over the world today still do this. Shelters around the world come in all shapes and sizes and are built of materials close on hand. On tropical islands, homes are built of palm fronds, bamboo, woven reeds, and thatched grasses. If there is a lot of clay or mud available then the homes are probably made from clay and mud. In the land that is barren, nomads have made shelters like yurts that are made of cloth and skeletal poles they can erect and dismantle as needed. You get the idea.

The science of home building is also a battle with gravity like the towers. Even if the structure is one story it must be able to support a roof with wide enough spaces beneath to allow rooms to fit different types of furnishings, such as bedrooms, bathrooms, and kitchens. There are other science principles like natural lighting that will not pertain to the STEM challenges, but might be worth mentioning. Energy efficient homes may face the south or west and windows are double paned. Earthquake areas also put extra safety features in houses to withstand shaking ground. Wet areas put houses up on stilts. Homes that your students are probably more familiar with may be constructed from a variety of materials available through importing and trade.

The math of home building is everywhere. There are measurements of square area, ceiling height, and angles where walls and corners meet just to mention a few. Drawings that are used in the process of construction and show all of these measurements are called blueprints. These drawings show all the sides of the three-dimensional home as well as a bird's eye view of each floor. The constraints and criteria of each house challenge will include measurements.

An architect is a person who develops the creative designs for buildings, homes, or other structures. So, the jobs of an engineer and architect are similar. The architect is more concerned with the look of the structure, whereas the engineer is more concerned with the safety and functionality of the structure. The engineer figures out which materials to use and how to safely construct the building the architect has envisioned. The difference between an architect and an engineer is that an architect focuses more on the artistry and design of the building, while the engineer focuses more on the technical and structural side. An engineer takes the blueprint presented by an architect and determines whether or not it is possible to build the structure, and the best materials to use. Different materials have different advantages, such as greater strength or greater flexibility.

Younger students K-2 or even older students that lack engineering experience will enjoy the first challenge that is modeled after the three famous pig brothers that set out into the world and had different ideas of how to build a house.

Example: **The Three Pigs House STEM Challenge** starts with a **House of Straw**

K-2 ETS 1-1 Ask questions, make observations, and gather information about a situation people want to change to define a simple problem that can be solved through the development of a new or improved object or tool.
K-2 ETS 1-2 Develop a simple sketch, drawing, or physical model to illustrate how the shape of an object helps it function as needed to solve a given problem.
K-2 ETS 1-3 Analyze data from tests of two objects designed to solve the same problem to compare the strengths and weaknesses of how each performs.

Material: 6 inches of masking tape, 2 pieces of construction paper, 20 drinking straws, and a floor fan to test

Safety: Only turn the fan on when the team is ready to test their house, then stay clear of the wind path.

Problem-> Imagine-> Design-> Create-> Test-> Analyze

Problem: There is a story about three little pigs that learned how important it is to build a house from sturdy material in order to keep the big bad wolf out. The problem for the first little pig is that there are only straws available. How can you build a house that is at least eight inches tall and at least eight inches wide using only straws and six inches of masking tape that has a paper roof and can withstand the winds of a fan for one minute?
Imagine what aerodynamic things allow wind to blow over them with less friction
Design by drawing your ideas on paper what a house could look like using just the materials available then collaborate with your team to discuss all ideas to combine them into a team blueprint.
Create by building the straw house following the criteria listed in the problem
Test by placing the finished house twelve inches in front of the fan. Each team can test their houses twice before the final test is done in front of all teams. The final test will be with the teacher measuring the height and width of the house and making sure there is a paper roof. If it is at least eight inches tall and wide then it will be placed on the test site which is 12 inches in front of the fan. If its roof stays on and doesn't move try the next speed on the fan until it does move or lasts one minute. If all houses moved then the one that moved the least is the strongest.
Analyze the house each time it is set in front of the fan to see how it is affected in order to address any design flaws and make improvements. After all houses have been tested analyze the different straw houses to compare the differences and similarities. Discuss the process each team used.

House Variation 1—**House of Sticks**

Material: 6 inches of masking tape, 2 pieces of copier paper, 20 Popsicle sticks (or sticks gathered on a nature walk) and a floor fan to test
Safety: Only turn the fan on when the team is ready to test their house, then stay clear of the wind path.

Problem-> Imagine-> Design-> Create-> Test-> Analyze

Problem: There is a story about three little pigs that learned how important it is to build a house from sturdy material in order to keep the big bad wolf out. The problem for the second little pig is that there is only sticks available. How can you build a house that is at least six inches tall and at least six inches wide using only sticks and six inches of masking tape that has a paper roof and can withstand the winds of a fan for one minute?
Imagine what aerodynamic things allow wind to blow over them with less friction
Design by drawing your ideas on paper what a house could look like using just the materials available then collaborate with your team to discuss all ideas to combine them into a team blueprint.
Create by building the stick house following the criteria listed in the problem
Test by placing the finished house twelve inches in front of the fan. Each team can test their houses twice before the final test is done in front of all teams. The final test will be with the teacher measuring the height and width of the house and making sure there is a paper roof. If it is at least eight inches tall and wide then it will be placed on the test site which is 12 inches in front of the fan. If its roof stays on and doesn't move try the next speed on the fan until it does move or lasts one minute. If all houses moved then the one that moved the least is the strongest.
Analyze the house each time it is set in front of the fan to see how it is affected in order to address any design flaws and make improvements. After all houses have been tested analyze the different stick houses to compare the differences and similarities. Discuss the process each team used. How did the stick house behave differently than the straw house?

House Variation 2—**House of Bricks**

Material: 6 inches of masking tape, 3 pieces of any kind paper, bricks (whatever is available and divided evenly between the teams, for example Jenga blocks or Lego bricks) and a floor fan to test

Safety: Only turn the fan on when the team is ready to test their house, then stay clear of the wind path.

Problem-> Imagine-> Design-> Create-> Test-> Analyze

Problem: There is a story about three little pigs that learned how important it is to build a house from sturdy material in order to keep the big bad wolf out. The problem for the third little pig is that there is only bricks available. How can you build a house that is at least ten inches tall and at least ten inches wide using only bricks and six inches of masking tape that has a paper roof and can withstand the winds of a fan for one minute?
Imagine what aerodynamic things allow wind to blow over them with less friction
Design by drawing your ideas on paper what a house could look like using just the materials available then collaborate with your team to discuss all ideas to combine them into a team blueprint.
Create by building the brick house following the criteria listed in the problem
Test by placing the finished house twelve inches in front of the fan. Each team can test their houses twice before the final test is done in front of all teams. The final test will be with the teacher measuring the height and width of the house and making sure there is a paper roof. If it is at least ten inches tall and wide then it will be placed

on the test site which is 12 inches in front of the fan. If its roof stays on and doesn't move try the next speed on the fan until it does move or lasts one minute. If all houses moved then the one that moved the least is the strongest. **Analyze** the house each time it is set in front of the fan to see how it is affected in order to address any design flaws and make improvements. After all houses have been tested analyze the different brick houses to compare the differences and similarities. Discuss the process each team used. Compare all the materials that have been used in the house builds.

For older students there can be more criteria added to the Pig House Challenge such as a house must contain a window and a working door.

House Variation 3—on Earth Day try the **Recycled Housing STEM Challenge.**

ETS1-1. Define a simple design problem reflecting a need or a want that includes specified criteria for success and constraints on materials, time, or cost.
ETS1-2. Generate and compare multiple possible solutions to a problem based on how well each is likely to meet the criteria and constraints of the problem.
ETS1-3. Plan and carry out fair tests in which variables are controlled and failure points are considered to identify aspects of a model or prototype that can be improved.

Material: any found or recycled material, glue or tape, a ruler

Safety: when using things from a recycling bin make sure there are no sharp edges and remove any food particles

Problem: People create new uses of old materials to help the economy and the environment at the same time. These conservation solutions are unique one-of-a-kind structures. They are made from waste normally thrown away to pile up in a dump to help save earth and money. 1.3 billion tons of solid waste that ends up in landfills could be turned into cheap, durable, and clean building materials. Your challenge is to design a prototype of a house from recycled or found material that has at least one window, one door that will open and close and a roof. Its dimensions must be at least 20 cm x 20 cm x 20 cm.
Imagine: There are houses made of tires, glass, plastic bottles, etc. There are some that even further save electricity and water and follow an Earthship concept. You may want to look for examples on the internet, but remember yours is just a prototype
Design: Look at your available material and draw some ideas out that incorporate the criteria from the problem
Create: Build your house prototype. Keep in mind that you may use cardboard to represent tires or plastic but explain that to your team and at testing
Test: When the building time is over go over the criteria and be able to show the window, demonstrate a working door, and have the correct dimensions and a roof
Analyze: Discuss the ideas that the team struggled with and how they overcame problems as a team.

In the discourse following any of the house challenges you should revisit the 4 C's. Ask for examples from students or point out the moments you observed while teams followed the design process. What is one example of creativity in this challenge? What is an example of good communication? What is an example of good collaboration? During the analyze step we hear a lot of examples of critical thinking, but what happened during the test, redesign, and retest that illustrates critical thinking?

The Recycled House would be a great challenge to revisit the 4C's because there is a lot of room for creativity when recycled and found materials are used. There is a need for more collaboration and critical thinking when the task is more complicated. Ask for examples of good communication in your discourse following the challenges.

Chapter 13
Solar Cookers

This category solar cookers involves food, so follow any guidelines your school or district enforce. It requires sunlight and may need to be done one challenge at a time throughout the year on sunny days. Seasons and holidays are suggested in each challenge. For example, one melts chocolate kisses and would be good for Valentine's Day. Another involves hot dogs and would be good for baseball season. Here is some background information before you begin.

Solar energy is the cleanest and most abundant renewable energy source available. You can use solar energy to reduce energy bills and save nonrenewable energy resources. The amount of sunlight that hits the earth's surface in an hour is enough to handle the entire world's energy consumption for a year, if only it could be captured. Solar technologies convert sunlight into electrical energy either through photovoltaic (PV) panels or through mirrors that concentrate solar radiation. This energy can be converted to electricity or stored in batteries or thermal storage.

Solar radiation is light or electromagnetic radiation emitted by the sun. While every location on Earth receives some sunlight over a year, the amount of solar radiation that reaches any one spot on the Earth's surface varies. There are several factors besides the tilt and location of the planet itself that affect that amount, topography, and cloud coverage, natural and manmade obstructions. Solar technologies capture this radiation and turn it into useful forms of energy.

People use solar thermal energy systems to heat water for homes, buildings, or swimming pools. People use solar energy to heat the inside of homes, greenhouses, and other buildings. Many electric companies are promoting solar conversion to power homes. Many car companies are now making EV's or electric vehicles. Tesla is a car company that devotes its engineering to the idea of electric cars.

Solar energy's main benefits are that air pollutants or carbon dioxide are not produced and their systems don't hurt the environment. Solar energy also has some limitations depending on location, time of day, and weather conditions; it is not constant. The amount of sunlight reaching a square foot of the earth's surface is small, so a large surface area is necessary to absorb or collect a useful amount of energy.

One early solar energy collection device was the solar oven (a box for collecting and absorbing sunlight). In the 1830s, British astronomer John Herschel used a solar oven to cook food during a trip to Africa. A solar cooker provides a passive option to prepare food using sunlight. A shoebox solar oven or cooker is easy to build using common household materials. The sun's rays are captured in the cooker, resulting in a temperature of 250 degrees Fahrenheit or more. Studies show that a temperature of 52 degrees C (125 degrees F) can cause a full-thickness skin burn in 2 minutes and a temperature of 54 degrees C (130 degrees F) can result in a full-thickness skin burn in 30 seconds. So keep that in mind when trying to heat different surfaces. If you are having students sit outside in the sunlight for any amount of time use sunscreen and other types of protection.

The sun is the fuel so solar cookers work best on sunny days and out of the wind. A solar cooker needs 3 things. A space to place the food, which can be a skewer, pan, plate, etc. Second, a way to trap the sunlight. You want the sun's rays to get in to heat the air, and not let the air out like a window made of plastic. Third, you need a reflector, something shiny to direct the sun's rays into the window or some color that absorbs as much heat as possible.

Review with students that air is made of matter because it has mass and takes up space. Because it is invisible to the naked eye, air is not an apparent factor in this challenge. The fact that electromagnetic energy can travel through clear material like windows allows it to transfer its radiant energy onto anything on the other side of the window. Then it heats up the matter inside any container enclosed by the windows. Use the analogy of a car in the summer. With the windows up in the heat, the air is trapped inside. When you open the door a blast of hot air greets you because the sunshine got through the windows and heated up everything inside the car including the air. Air is matter and its molecules get heated up along with all the solid things you can easily see inside the car and likewise inside a solar cooker.

It is not necessary to have a thermometer for this STEM challenge, but it is a great way to include more science and math if readily available. A thermometer is an instrument that measures temperature. It can measure the temperature of a solid such as food, a liquid such as water, or a gas such as air. The three most common units of measurement for temperature are Celsius, Fahrenheit, and kelvin. The Celsius scale is part of the metric system. The metric system of measurement also includes units of mass, such as kilograms, and units of length, such as kilometers. The metric system, including Celsius, is the official system of measurement for almost all countries in the world. Most scientific fields measure temperature using the Celsius scale. Zero degrees Celsius is the freezing point of water, and 100 degrees Celsius is the boiling point of water. Three nations do not use the Celsius scale. The United States, Burma, and Liberia use the Fahrenheit scale to measure temperature.

However, even in these countries, scientists use the Celsius or Kelvin scale to measure temperature. Water freezes at 32 degrees Fahrenheit and boils at 212 degrees Fahrenheit. The Kelvin scale is used by physicists and other scientists who need to record very precise temperatures. The Kelvin scale is the only unit of measurement to include the temperature for "absolute zero," the total absence of any heat energy. A meat thermometer is a small, prong-type device that measures the internal temperatures of meats that you may have on hand, but you do not need to go out and buy one for this challenge.

Example: **Solar Cookers STEM Challenge-**
S'mores Solar Cooker
I can build a solar cooker from found materials that will melt the marshmallow

3-5-ETS1-1. Define a simple design problem reflecting a need or a want that includes specified criteria for success and constraints on materials, time, or cost.
3-5-ETS1-2. Generate and compare multiple possible solutions to a problem based on how well each is likely to meet the criteria and constraints of the problem.
3-5-ETS1-3. Plan and carry out fair tests in which variables are controlled and failure points are considered to identify aspects of a model or prototype that can be improved.

Materials: Each group gets aluminum foil, plastic wrap, scissors, tape, glue, black construction paper, sticks, and a box or empty container. Find a recycled box, such as a shoebox, pizza box, or Pringle's can

Safety: Use scissors safely.
　　　　Wear sunscreen and/or hat if staying outside with the cooker in the sun.
　　　　When handling food that will be eaten use gloves and if it falls to the ground it is trash.

Problem: We need an alternative way to cook food since energy is limited.
Imagine solutions by thinking of solar cookers you have used, seen, or built
Design: each team member draws a plan on white paper for a solar cooker.
Share **plans** and note the good ideas of each to combine into a team endeavor.
Create solar cookers: Some teams may line the inside of their container with aluminum foil to reflect sunlight or line some sides with black construction paper to absorb heat. There should be a transparent window of some

sort so the sun rays can get inside the box to heat up the air molecules inside the cooker. Teams could cover the entire top of a shoebox or pizza box or cut small windows and cover with plastic wrap and tape into place.

Test: Find an open sunny area, preferably outside, to set up cookers. Place marshmallows inside the cooker and begin the timer. Check the status of the marshmallows every 30-60 minutes until they are melty enough to become S'mores with graham crackers and chocolate chips. The meltiest wins, but since everyone gets to eat a s'more everyone feels like a winner.

Analyze: Compare each solar cooker and discuss the strengths and weaknesses. Which cookers melted the marshmallows the quickest? Were the larger ones with more air inside better or worse? Why do you believe this is so? Were ones with larger windows better or worse? Why do you believe this is so?

Redesign and retest.

Variations

Different materials make each cooker construction a new challenge. Because it touches food, any part that has contact needs to be thrown away and replaced when iterations happen.

Solar Cooker Variation 1—**Valentine Cooker** (or **Sloppy Kiss** if you aren't censored)

To celebrate Valentine's you could have a Sloppy Kiss contest by trying to melt Hershey Kisses the quickest in solar cookers. There should be as many kisses as there are team members and should be unwrapped partially so that the chocolate is exposed, but sitting on its wrapper instead of the cooker for easier handling. Remember the melting point of chocolate falls between 86°F and 90°F. This is lower than the average temperature of the human body, which is 98.6°F so the heat from your hand raises the temperature of the chocolate and causes it to melt. You must be able to see the inside of the cooker in order to see when it melts and before it gets too messy for extraction.

Problem-> Imagine-> Design-> Create-> Test-> Analyze

Problem: There is a fun contest to see who can create a solar cooker that will melt chocolate the quickest

Imagine what materials feel warm to the touch. If it is warm to your hand then it is warmer than your body temperature, but be aware that the skin on your hand can be colder than the rest of your body due to its distance from the heart and the increased surface area exposure to outside temperature. People that use their body to gauge the temperature of material always risk being burned as well.

Design by drawing a solar cooker with material available that would include a way to see inside the cooker so that the first sign of melting can be detected.

Create by building the solar cooker large enough for four chocolate kisses to safely sit inside

Test by bringing each team's solar cooker to the area with sun exposure and set the timer

Analyze the differences in the cookers and the process that each team used in the creation. Enjoy the sloppy kisses and have a Happy Valentine's Day!

Solar Cooker Variation 2—**Hot Dog!**

To celebrate the start of baseball season you could have hot dogs and buns heated up with solar cookers. The design process is the same, but no one wants to eat a cold hot dog, so there needs to be a backup plan in case the time needed to cook the hot dogs is not long enough or the sun not hot enough. It is definitely the last iteration so that teams can utilize all they have learned to create the optimum solar cooker. Since the shape of the hot dog is a long cylinder you should start collecting tube shaped objects like Pringles cans, paper towel tubes, water bottles, etc. to be the cookers, but with smaller volume of cookers and larger volume of food item then every student could cook their own.

Again, the handling of food that will be eaten should be considered and monitored. Hot dogs are ready when they reach an internal temperature of at least 140°F. It's always a good idea to keep an instant-read thermometer close by when cooking, meat thermometers from home would be great if available. Some hot dogs are safe to eat cold, while others are not. The best way to know more about your hot dog is to check the label of the packaging they are sold in. If the hot dogs are fully cooked when sold, they are fine to eat cold. The labeling will also give you good information for other factors—such as safe handling, the cooking instructions, and the ingredients and nutrient contents. Most handling requires the hot dogs to be kept cold in the fridge, even if they are fully cooked, partially cooked, or raw. If the labeling says the hot dogs are partially cooked or raw, you should avoid eating them cold. They might contain bacteria and other nasties that could cause food poisoning and other illnesses. These should always be cooked before consumption and be eaten right away.

Problem-> Imagine-> Design-> Create-> Test-> Analyze

Problem: There is a need for a solar hot dog cooker are you up to the challenge?
Imagine what other hot dog cookers like the ones at gas stations look like. Most have heat lamps, but you are using sunshine instead
Design by drawing a model of the prototype using the available recycled materials. Meet as team to look at the drawings and discuss the best parts to combine into a team mode.
Create by building the solar cookers
Test by bringing each team's hot dog cookers to the area with abundant sunshine and using a thermometer if available to see which hot dogs got the warmest.
Analyze the differences in the solar cookers and what some of the advantages and disadvantages there are to solar cooking.

The solar cookers would be a great challenge to revisit the 4C's because there is a lot of room for creativity when recycled and found materials are used. There is a need for more collaboration and critical thinking when the task is more complicated. Ask for examples of good communication in your discourse following the challenges. Always take notes during the challenges knowing what you wish to highlight during the analysis step.

Solar Cooker Variation 3—**Say Cheese**
Add a bowl and cheese to the solar cooker materials list and follow the design process

Problem-> Imagine-> Design-> Create-> Test-> Analyze

Problem: Another popular concession stand food is nachos or pretzels with cheese. There is a need for a solar cooker to melt cheese are you up to the challenge?
Imagine what other devices melt cheese, but remember you are using sunshine instead
Design by drawing a model of the prototype using the available recycled materials. Meet as team to look at the drawings and discuss the best parts to combine into a team mode.
Create by building the solar cookers
Test by bringing each team's cheese solar cookers to the area with abundant sunshine.
Analyze the differences in the solar cookers and what some of the advantages and disadvantages there are to solar cooking.

Bring some tortilla chips or pretzels in and start pouring the cheese on instead of dipping. Each team member should get a plate of their choice of either chips or pretzels and you should divide the cheese up equally among the team members.

Solar Cookers

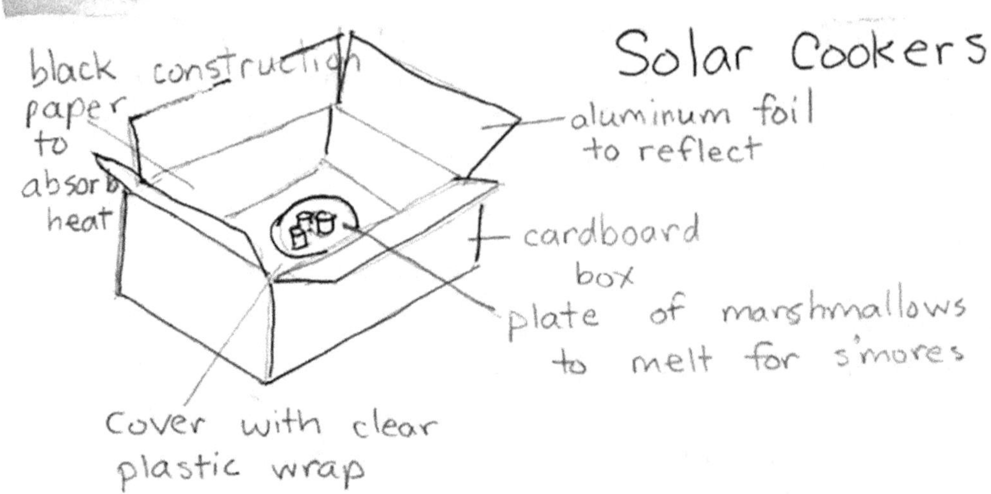

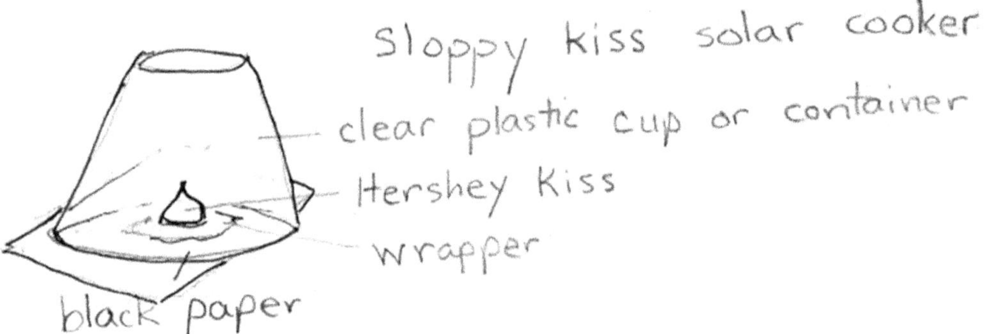

Hot Dog Cooker

Chapter 14
Student Resources

79

Name________________________________ Date________________

The design I plan for our prototype:

____

Data from the Test step:

Ideas to remember for the Analysis discussion (continue on the back as needed):

Name _________________________ Date _______________

Draw a picture, create a definition, or give examples for each team skill.

Collaboration means:

Communication means:

Creativity means:
Critical Thinking means:

The Engineering Design Process:

Problem->

Imagine->

81

Design->

Create->

Test->

Analyze->

Teacher Resources

Possible Road Map for Implementing STEM in a Nine-Month School Year

Perhaps you have taken a STEM workshop or just read a few articles, but now that you have read this book you are really ready to begin!

Month 1 (August or September depending on your school year)

Set up a materials area and start collecting recycled and inexpensive supplies, see pages 15-16

Create or purchase an engineering design process poster to display in the classroom, see page 4

Create or purchase Accountable Talk protocols or stems, see pages 34-35

Use hands-on lesson Paper Chains to teach the process and team skills, see chapter 4

Use hands-on lesson Pipe Cleaner Tower to review the skills, see chapter 4

Have students make posters or complete the worksheet to illustrate Collaboration, Creativity, Communication, and Critical Thinking

Month 2: TOWERS

Begin challenges chapters and go in any order you wish, but this plan will go in the order of the book

Read the background information about towers, see chapter 5

Have a Tallest Tower stations day using materials available in the classroom, see page 55

Get spaghetti and marshmallows

Week 2 Run the Spaghetti Tower challenge

Week 3 run a variation using new materials like straws and tape to build an apartment building prototype

Week 4 run a variation using new materials like pencils and clay to build a lighthouse prototype

Future week possibly in December—revisit using toothpicks and gumdrops to build a holiday sculpture

Month 3: CARS

Read the background information about cars, see chapter 6

Run the Wind-Powered Car challenge

Week 2 run a variation using new materials and gravity like a Cars and Ramps challenge

Week 3 run a variation using potential energy like the Rubber band Car challenge

Week 4 run a variation using Balloons for energy to move the car

Month 4: BOATS

Read the background information about boats, see chapter 7

Collect pennies to represent passengers

Run the Foil Boats challenge

Week 2 run a variation of the Boat challenge using clay or playdough

Week 3 run a variation of the Boat challenge using new materials like craft sticks and tape

Week 4 run a variation either Sailboat or Pontoon boat challenge

Month 5: BRIDGES
Read the background information about bridges, see chapter 8
Run the Paper Beam Bridge challenge
Week 2 run a variation creating a Truss Bridge from straws and tape
Week 3 run a variation of the bridge challenge using cotton swabs (Bone Bridge) and tape or craft sticks
Week 4 run a variation creating a Suspension Bridge or a Pontoon Bridge from recycled material

Month 6: CATAPULTS
Read the background information about bridges, see chapter 9
Run the Catapult Challenge with foil balls or pompons for distance
Week 2 run a variation hitting a target
Week 3 run a variation kicking a football through the uprights with precision of a Football Catapult
Week 4 run a variation using a catapult to sink baskets with a Basketball Catapult

Month 7: PLANES
Read the background information, see chapter 10
Begin with Penny Passenger Airplanes challenge with paper airplanes
Week 2 run a variation with a straw as the fuselage for the planes with Straw Gliders
Week 3 run a variation with a straw and rings as the wings and tail for Ring Flyers
Week 4 run a variation creating a slingshot launcher for the paper airplanes

Month 8: MARBLE MAZES
Read the background information about marble mazes, see chapter 11
Run the Paper Plate Maze Challenge
Week 2 run the variation using recycled material for a 30 Second Marble Maze Challenge
Week 3 run the variation creating a Miniature Mini-Golf Hole
Week 4 run the variation to increase the 30 second maze to 60 seconds

Month 9: HOUSES
Read the background information about houses, see chapter 12
Begin the Three Pigs Challenge
Week 1 create houses of straw
Week 2 create houses of sticks
Week 3 create houses of bricks
Week 4 run the Recycled House Challenge—this would be a good one to run on Earth Day (April 22)

Month 10: SOLAR COOKERS
Read the background information about solar cookers, see chapter 13
Begin with the S'mores Solar Cooker Challenge to melt a marshmallow
Week 2 run a variation to melt a Hershey Kiss (I like to call it Sloppy Kiss, but I know that may get some heat from administration—no pun intended)
Week 3 run a variation to cook hot dogs in time for some baseball
Week 4 run a variation to melt cheese for pretzels

Another option: NATIVE AMERICAN ENGINEERING
Read the background information about First Nations before each challenge to learn about how Native Americans solved their real-world problems with engineering.
Begin with the Totem Pole challenge

Week 2 the Teepee challenge has teams creating a prototype of a type dwelling that will withstand the wind on the plains (a fan)

Week 3 the bow and arrow challenge shoots for distance or accuracy with potential energy of the bow and bowstring transferring energy to the arrow

Week 4 the canoes will be made of clay instead of wood to hold the most cargo

The Engineering Design Process for a Topic of Your Choice

Title

Background Information

Math Concepts that apply

Science Concepts that apply

Materials needed

Problem->

Imagine->

Design->

Create->

Test->

Analyze->

Chapter 15
Additional/Optional Activities

There are several schools that are in session longer than nine months. There are teachers that teach summer school. There are some faint of heart that do not want to attempt the Boat chapter. There are some that now love STEM so much they want some extra activities to do at home with their own children during summer vacation. For all of you, I am including some additional or optional STEM activities. I hope you have a blast with these challenges.

These will be a different theme altogether. Totally different. You could do iterations of the four different challenges and make it last several months, but I wanted to include four totally unique challenges instead of iterations of just one. The theme is Native American Engineering and the challenges include totems, teepees, crossbows, and canoes. The theme may not suit many, but it is an alternative for any that did not want to do one of the original nine. Maybe your area does not have enough sunshine or high enough temperatures to do the solar cooker unit, so now you have an alternative.

These STEM challenges are not meant to be culturally offensive to anyone and I have nothing but respect and admiration for the First Nations of North America. As a teacher I celebrated November as National Native American Heritage Month since 1990 when President Bush signed the proclamation. I had actually been teaching about the different contributions of the first Americans for ten years before that. My dad loved finding arrowheads in freshly plowed fields along riverbanks and had a huge collection of artifacts which I borrowed to display. He claimed that our family had Cherokee ancestors, but that has never been proven.

I believe these challenges would fit in nicely during the month of November or one at a time as they fit into your schedule. For example, Columbus Day in October is now widely known as Indigenous Peoples' Day instead and it would be appropriate to do one of these STEM challenges that day.

Because of the diversity of Native American tribes, I include background for each activity instead of one blanket introduction. Not every tribe had totem poles. Not every tribe had teepees. Not every tribe had bows or canoes. That is one problem with prejudice and racism is that people lump all of one race together and make assumptions. For example, many assume that all Indians slept in teepees or hunted with a bow and arrows. Those ideas hopefully will be debunked when you share the background information before each challenge. Cultural awareness and appreciation are my goal. I want students to see how each tribe was able to solve their real-world problems with engineering.

Native American Engineering #1

Totem Poles

Background information

Totem poles are monuments that were created by First Nations of the Pacific Northwest to represent and commemorate ancestry, histories, people, or events. They are one of the most recognizable cultural symbols of the Pacific Northwest. There is an array of different totem pole styles and designs. Totems were erected for welcoming, memorializing, building, and sometimes even shaming. Carving a totem pole requires artistic skill, and an understanding of cultural histories and forest ecology. Before a cedar tree is harvested for a totem pole, many coastal First Nations communities performed a ceremony of gratitude and respect in honor of the tree. The tradition of the totem poles existed from the southeast corners of Alaska through British Columbia, Canada all the way to western parts of Washington.

Totem poles stand between 3 to 18 meters tall, but some have been found that are over 20 meters in height. Different types of totem poles were built to serve various architectural and ceremonial purposes. Most longhouses had house posts, carved with human or animal forms, to support the main beams of the building. Some stand alone.

Most totem poles are made from western red cedar, a rot-resistant tree that is straight-grained and easy to carve. Even though it resists rotting most will disintegrate in two hundred years, so the few that still exist are treasures and are being preserved. Carvings on the totem poles included birds, fish, animals, insects, plants and humans, but also other animals called shapeshifters like the thunderbird that were sent by the Gods to protect humans from evil. Common animals carved on totems were the wolf, eagle, grizzly bear, killer whale, frog, raven, and salmon. Rich and important families used their totems like a crest to show they were related to certain clans and ancestors. Totem poles can also be created to honor a particular event or important person.

After a tree is chopped down, the bark is stripped off, and then the wood is shaped using tools such as adzes, axes, chisels, carving knives, and chainsaws. Sometimes it is then painted using natural pigments.

Totem Pole STEM Challenge

Problem: The longhouse is a shelter made from long poles formed from tall red cedar trees that grew all over the Northwest. The longhouse needed to have a central post to support the main beams of the building. The supporting vertical post that was at the entrance to the longhouse was decorated with carvings of the family crest and have become known as totem poles.

You are trying to build the tallest totem pole with only **one piece of construction paper, 2 pieces of copy paper, crayons, markers, glue, scissors, and 12 inches of tape** that will display your 3 crests.

Imagine: It may help to think about towers and how they were constructed with a wider base in order to go up while not falling over.

Design: Plan a prototype of a totem pole depicting emblems that represent each team member. Each member can draw their own or tell the most artistic member what they want drawn. This step should take only about five minutes individually and then five more as a team.

Create: Teams will have fifteen minutes to construct their totem pole with the materials available.

Test: When time is called the totem poles will be measured and then each team will have five minutes to make design changes or additions. When time is called again the totem poles will be measured once again.

Analyze: Analyze the totem poles. Get the teams together to analyze together. Compare and contrast the team's choices of animals and shapes on their crests. Discuss the process each team employed. Then decide why the tallest totem was able to achieve its height.

Review the 4 C's and ask for examples the students felt exhibited each skill throughout their process. Ask for examples of creativity, collaboration, communication, and critical thinking.

Native American Engineering #2

Teepees

Background Information

Native Americans lived in a wide variety of homes. Different tribes and peoples built different types of homes. The kinds of homes they lived in was dependent on the materials that they had readily available where they lived. It also depended on the kind of lifestyle they lived as well as the environment.

Some tribes were nomads. This means the entire village would travel from place to place and camp. This was common for tribes living in the Great Plains where they hunted buffalo for food. The tribe would follow the large buffalo herds as they roamed the plains. These tribes built homes that were easy to move and build.

Other tribes lived in one place for a long time. This was because they had water and food nearby. These tribes built more permanent homes like the pueblo or longhouse.

Plains Indians, such as, Lakota, Pawnee, Arapahoe, Kiowah, and Cheyenne tribes, moved from place to place throughout the year, so their shelters were lightweight, collapsible structures called teepees or tipis. This cone shaped tent was made by stretching buffalo skin over a frame of 20-30 sapling poles that leaned into each other and were tied at the top. There was a flap at the top to let the smoke from the cooking fire exit and a flap at the bottom that was a door for people to exit and enter. In the summer the covering would be raised to allow for a large gap at the bottom. This gap let air flow through the teepee and keep the inside cool.

Teepee STEM Challenge

This challenge is for you to design a teepee that will resist wind gusts of the Great Plains to stay upright.

Materials: one large piece of construction paper or cloth, 8-12 craft sticks or skewers or pencils, 6 inches of string, scissors, and 6 inches of tape

Problem: The Plains tribes needed to be able to pack up everything including their house to take with them to the next camp as they followed the buffalo their main food source across the plains. They needed the type of mobile shelter that could be folded up and carried.

Imagine: You are trying to build a tent structure strong enough to withstand the wind gusts that blow across the plains. Teepees of the past were circular at the bottom and resembled a cone, but could it have a square or triangular base like pyramids?

Design: Plan a prototype of a teepee using the materials available

Create: Teams will have fifteen minutes to construct their teepee with the materials available.

Test: When time is called the teepees will be tested one at a time in front of a fan with its speed increased at 30 second intervals until the teepee either moves or withstands the wind and remains in one spot. Then each team will have five minutes to make design changes or additions. When time is called again the teepees will be tested.

Analyze: Analyze the teepees. Get the teams together to analyze together. Compare and contrast the team's structures. Discuss the process each team employed. Then decide what enabled the teepees to withstand the winds. Review the 4 C's and ask for examples the students felt exhibited each skill throughout their process. Ask for examples of creativity, collaboration, communication and critical thinking.

Native American Engineering #3

Bow and Arrow

Background Information

Bows and arrows were made by Native Americans using whatever local natural resources and raw materials were available to them. A tough, hard, flexible wood could make the bows like, ash, hickory, oak, cedar, walnut and birch. The wood had to be strong enough to be flexed and pulled repeatedly without getting brittle or snapping in two. They were usually about a yard in length. Horns, antlers or the bones of large animals, like from the rib cage of the buffalo or whale, could also be used to make bows. Thicker in the middle to make it stronger and provide a handle. Notches cut at both ends made anchors for the bowstring.

Bowstrings were made of animal gut, sinew or rawhide. Sometimes plant fibers were used for drawstrings like milkweed, and dogbane or the inner bark of basswood or yucca. Materials like these that were flexible and tough to string from the ends of the bow.

Arrow shafts were made from reeds or shoots that were half as long as the bow. The ends were both notched to attach a point and to glide onto the bowstring. Arrowheads were made by chipping a stone or bone into a point with sharp edges all the way around and lashed to the shaft. Later arrows had metal arrowheads after trade with Europeans began. Feathers were also lashed to the other end to make it fly straight. The art of making efficient weapons with bows and arrows required balance and engineering.

Bows and arrows are the most recognized weapon of Native American Indians and were used for hunting and fighting. Bows and arrows are long range and accurate and could be used for rapid shots on foot or on horseback. Bows for horseback riders were smaller than those used on foot since a rider is sitting.

There are physics involved in shooting with a bow and arrow that should be kept in mind when constructing them. A bow acts like a double spring. When pulled by the string it deforms the original shape and will snap back into place when released. The bowstring may be a little elastic, but needs to be able to pull the bow back and will store the potential energy equal to the force pulling it back and then transfers it to the arrow. The arrow becomes a projectile which follows a trajectory until it hits a target or is pulled back to earth with gravity. The harder the string is pulled, the farther an arrow will fly. To increase its range, an arrow is usually shot upward and will follow an arc path.

Keep in mind that bows are not straight. It might be a good idea to read this background information to the students and let them have overnight to scout possible things to use for the bow from home, outdoors, and around recycling bins. I have used clothes hangers both wire and plastic with adaptations. I have had students bring in toys from the dollar store; you will have to decide if you would allow that. If your school is around any wooded area, it would be a great outdoor classroom project to scout for fallen limbs and sticks to fashion into bows and smaller ones for arrows.

The challenge is written with materials I have used, but can be done on a much larger scale with more iterations, depending on what you have available. There is engineering involved in the construction and design of the bow, of the arrow, and of how it is shot.

Bow and Arrow STEM Challenge

Material: clothes hangers, straws, string, rubber bands, masking tape, clear tape, yarn, scissors, feathers, pencil top erasers

Decide if the goal is distance or accuracy. Distance is measuring and accuracy requires a target.

Problem: The Plains tribes needed to be able to hunt for food because trapping takes time and these tribes were not in one place for very long. The hunting needed to be able to be done on foot or from horseback. The device needed to be accurate because some game was small like rabbit and some fast like deer. Can you make an accurate bow and arrow?

Imagine: You are trying to make a bow and arrow. Think of ones you have seen in pictures or in person and what kind of materials were used.

Design: Plan a prototype if your bow must be made from a clothes hanger and arrow from a drinking straw. Look at the other materials available and draw your design to share with your team and combine the great ideas.

Create: Teams will have fifteen minutes to construct their bow and arrow with the materials available.

Test: When time is called the bow and arrow will be tested one at a time from a starting line for distance or to a target. No one should test by shooting anywhere but the designated area. Then each team will have ten minutes to make design changes or additions. When time is called again the bow and arrow will be tested. This test, analyze, redesign, and retest cycle can be run as long as time allows.

Analyze: Analyze the bow and arrows. Get the teams together to analyze together. Compare and contrast the team's devices. Discuss the process each team employed. Then decide what enabled the bow and arrow combination that went the farthest or which bow and arrow combination was the most accurate. Review the 4 C's and ask for examples the students felt exhibited each skill throughout their process. Ask for examples of creativity, collaboration, communication and critical thinking.

Some ideas for targets are concentric circles like a dart board, but drawn with chalk on the playground or crayons on paper attached to a fence.

Native American Engineering #4

Canoes

Background information

Canoes are a type of boat, so the physics of buoyancy still apply. Remember from the boat chapter that buoyancy equals the weight of the liquid that an object displaces. If an object in water pushes aside an amount of water equal to the weight of the object (like a boat), it will float. If not, it will sink. Water exerts an upward force upon objects called the buoyant force. When the weight of an object is greater than the water's buoyant force, the object sinks. When the weight is less, the object floats, and when equal, the object will remain at a certain level in the water. The more surface area an object has, the more buoyant force it has being applied to it to help it float.

Canoes were very important to the Native Americans both for fishing and transportation. Since many of the Native American tribes lived near bodies of water like streams, rivers, lakes, and oceans, being able to fish was important. Fishing from canoes was done with spears and bows, or hooks that made from antlers or bones. Transportation was needed for times when trade with other tribes or cultures was necessary.

Most canoes were made of birch bark or dug out of other available trees cut in half and hollowed down the middle. Canoes were built in different sizes. Records show that there were boats built for one person, and boats that could hold up to 50 people at once. The average lengths were between 10 and 24 feet long. Most canoes were small, light, and fast to carry a few people rapidly over rivers and lakes.

Canoes resemble Viking ships and appear in sketches hundreds of years old, but the older canoes did not make it because they are biodegradable and therefore rotted. Other rowboats have the paddler facing the rear of the boat, but in the canoe the paddler faces the direction of travel. The sides were high enough to keep out water waves and the ends taper and bow upward to a point to cut through the water. That shape has stayed the same for centuries.

Canoe STEM Challenge

Material: clay or playdough, pennies or marbles, scissors, toothpicks, molding tools, a tub to hold water, and paper towels to dry between tests

Problem: The Native Americans that lived near water wanted fish as a food source. To catch larger fish than those that swim in the shallow waters near shore they needed a way to get on the water and to deeper areas with bigger fish.

Imagine: Think of canoes you have seen in pictures or in person and how they looked and how they were used.

Design: Plan a prototype of your canoe. Look at the other materials available and draw your design to share with your team and combine the great ideas.

Create: Teams will have ten minutes to construct their canoe with the materials available.

Test: When time is called the canoes will be tested one at a time in the tub. First just to see if they float. Then they can be tested by adding fish, which is either pennies or marbles. The one that sank the canoe is not counted. Then each team will have ten minutes to make design changes or additions. When time is called again, the canoes will be retested. This test, analyze, redesign, and retest cycle can be run as long as time allows.

Analyze: Analyze the canoes. Get the teams together to analyze together. Compare and contrast the team's vessels. Discuss the process each team employed.

Review the 4 C's and ask for examples the students felt exhibited each skill throughout their process. Ask for examples of creativity, collaboration, communication and critical thinking.

Bibliography

Beyer, B. K. (1995) *Critical thinking*, Bloomington, IN: Phi Delta Kappa Educational Foundation.

Cherry, K. (2022) 'Understanding the Psychology of Creativity', *Very Well Mind.*
https://www.verywellmind.com/what-is-creativity-p2-3986725.

Cox, L. (2022) 'Who Invented the Car', *Live Science.* https://www.livescience.com/37538-who-invented-the-car.html.

Finio, B. (2022) 'Build a Paper Airplane Launcher', *Science Buddies.*
https://www.sciencebuddies.org/stem-activities/paper-airplane-launcher.

Ghose, T and Harvey, A. (2022) 'What is Friction', *Live Science.*
https://www.livescience.com/37161-what-is-friction.html.

Hanifan, O. (01/10/22) '5 Ways to Establish Effective Communication in the Classroom', *Mentimeter.*
https://www.mentimeter.com/blog/interactive-classrooms/5-ways-to-establish-effective-communication-in-the-classroom.

Harris, T. (12/20/22) 'How Skyscrapers Work', *How Stuff Works.*
https://science.howstuffworks.com/engineering/structural/skyscraper1.htm.

History.com editors. (2010) 'Norwegian ethnologist Thor Heyerdahl sails papyrus boat', *History.*
https://www.history.com/this-day-in-history/heyerdahl-sails-papyrus-boat.

HTHT editors. (2020) 'Medieval engineers: The science behind the catapult', *Science Made Fun.*
https://sciencemadefun.net/blog/medieval-engineers-the-science-behind-the-catapult/.

Huang, A. (2009) 'Totem Poles', *Indigenous Foundations.*
https://indigenousfoundations.arts.ubc.ca/totem_poles/.

Hunter Old Elk. (2017) 'Inside the Lodge: Plains Indian Tipis', *Buffalo Bill Center of the West.*
https://centerofthewest.org/2017/10/19/inside-the-lodge/.

Jaron. (10/03/22) 'Is it Safe to Eat Cold Hot Dogs? Complete Guide', *Foodsguy.* https://foodsguy.com/eat-cold-hot-dogs/.

Jasnani, P. (03/05/2022) 'Critical Thinking in Education', *Study.com.*
https://study.com/academy/lesson/teaching-critical-thinking-skills.

Jasnani, P. (05/20/22) 'Critical Thinking Skills', *Skills You Need*. Critical Thinking | SkillsYouNeed.

Lamb, R., Morrissey, M. and Kiger, P. (2021) 'How bridges work', *How Stuff Works*. https://science.howstuffworks.com/engineering/civil/bridge.htm.

May, S. (2018) 'Engineering Design Process', NASA. https://www.nasa.gov/audience/foreducators/best/edp.html

National Governors Association Center for Best Practices and Council of Chief State School Officers. (2010) College and Career Readiness Standards. https://new.ccea-nv.org/wp-content/uploads/2019/10/CCR-CCSS-Anchor-Standards.pdf.

Next Generation Science Standards. https://www.nextgenscience.org/dci-arrangement/hs-ets1-engineering-design.

'10 Strategies to Build on Student Collaboration in the Classroom', *The Graduate School of Education and Human Development*. (2017) https://gsehd.gwu.edu/articles/10-strategies-build-student-collaboration-classroom

Randle, A. (2021) 'History of Flight: Breakthroughs, Disasters, and More', *History*. https://www.history.com/news/history-flight-aviation-timeline.

'Solar Cookers', FSEC. https://energyresearch.ucf.edu/education/k-12/resources/solar-cookers/.

Stemler, S., Straten, M., Beggs, K., Lander, D., Watrous, A. and Yowell J. (2006) 'Architects and Engineers: Working Together to Design Structures.' *Teaching Engineering*. https://www.teachengineering.org/lessons/view/cub_intro_lesson03#:~:text=An%20architect%20and%20engine er%20both,%2C%20bridges%2C%20and%20other%20structures.

Taylor, L. (2022) 'How Did Native Americans Make Bows and Arrows', *The Classroom*. https://www.theclassroom.com/how-did-american-indians-make-bows-arrows-12078470.html.

Walsh, R. (2022) '25 Different Kinds of Houses from Around the World.' *Compassion*. https://www.compassionuk.org/blogs/25-different-types-of-houses-from-around-the-world/.

Woodford, C. (2021) 'Ships and Boats', *Explain That Stuff*. https://www.explainthatstuff.com/how-ships-work.html.